Duluth

The City and The People

by Chuck Frederick

American & World Geographic Publishing

*For Mom and Dad—who believed in me
long before I believed in myself.
Thanks.
And especially for Julie—my inspiration,
my best friend and the best copy editor I know.*

JACK RENDULICH

Text © 1994 Chuck Frederick
© 1994 Unicorn Publishing, Inc.

This book may not be reproduced in whole or in part by any means (with the exception of short quotes for the purpose of review) without the permission of the publisher.

Write for our catalog:
American & World Geographic Publishing, P. O. Box 5630, Helena, MT 59604
Printed in U.S.A. by Fenske Companies, Billings, Montana

Library of Congress Cataloging-in-Publication Data
Frederick, Chuck.
    Duluth : the city and the people / by Chuck Frederick.
        p.   cm.
    Includes bibliographical references and index
    ISBN 1-56037-068-8
    1. Duluth Minn.)–History. 2. Duluth (Minn.)–Geography. I. Title.
F614.D8F72 1994   94-26626
977.6'77–dc20

Above: *The Aerial Lift Bridge with autumn accessories.*
Facing page: *Appreciating Duluth from a Cessna 180.* LARRY MAYER

Title page: *A superior morning in Duluth-Superior Harbor.* BOB FIRTH

Front cover: *The city in formal evening attire.*
BOB FIRTH
Back cover, top: *A bird's-eye view.* LARRY MAYER
Bottom: *Typical traffic.* RICHARD HAMILTON SMITH

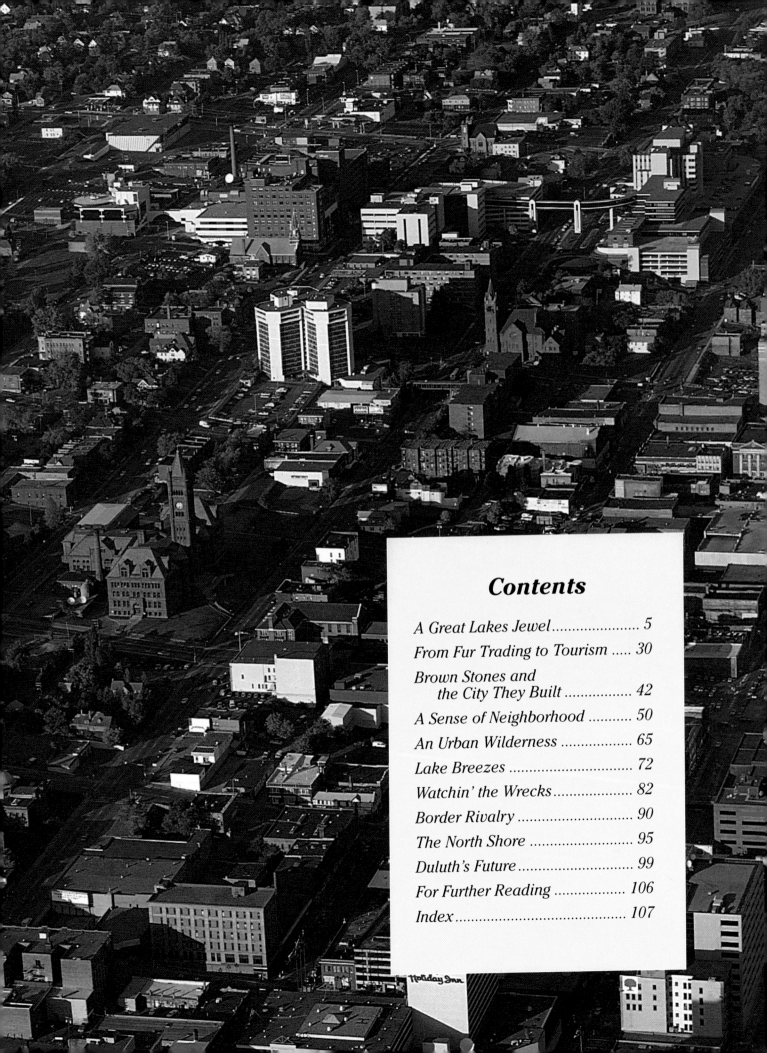

Contents

A Great Lakes Jewel 5

From Fur Trading to Tourism 30

Brown Stones and
    the City They Built 42

A Sense of Neighborhood 50

An Urban Wilderness 65

Lake Breezes 72

Watchin' the Wrecks 82

Border Rivalry 90

The North Shore 95

Duluth's Future 99

For Further Reading 106

Index 107

And for a celebration, add just a few more lights and colors.

A Great Lakes Jewel

Nose your car over the crest of the Duluth hillside and slow down a bit.

You probably won't be able to help yourself.

Stretched out in the still night, the breathtaking view of thousands of twinkling lights welcome you to a uniquely beautiful city, a city built between the edge of a wilderness and the rugged shores of the greatest of the Great Lakes.

Carved from a wooded hillside, Duluth stretches nearly as far as your eye can see. Look west from the top of the hill toward the working class neighborhoods that line the shores of the winding, tree-lined St. Louis River. Then look east toward the mansions that grace the rocky shoreline of Lake Superior.

But don't look away long. Those warm, friendly city lights that frame the corner of Lake Superior here in northeastern Minnesota are certain to hold your eyes' attention. No matter how many times you've seen them, they always stop you short.

There's nothing like that first time, though. So be sure to enjoy it. Wind your way slowly down the hill. Ease into the jewel of the Great Lakes.

Before there was a Duluth, the area was visited more than 200 years ago by voyagers, missionaries and explorers drawn here by an abundance of beaver pelts and lush forests.

The promise of a better life still calls people to this largely undiscovered region.

And though it's a city that has seen its share of boom-and-bust cycles—each one teaching the 85,000 or so people who live here how to persevere and how to survive—it's the ongoing realization of a better life that holds them here.

Duluthians have always dug in their heels during bad times. And during good times, during those years of economic prosperity, they've turned their corner of America into a showcase.

They've created a city that somehow gets under your skin and makes you feel at home, even if you're visiting only a short time.

It's hard to say how or why. And it's impossible to explain what it is that magically calls people here and pulls at them when they leave. But the magic is unmistakable. You can see it in the red and orange hues of a Lake Superior sunrise, or feel it in the spooky fog that rolls low off the lake, embracing the skyline but leaving downtown rooftops basked in sunlight.

Some have speculated the magic lies with the lake. More likely, though, it lies with the people.

It's the kind of place where folks don't hesitate to help each other. Where neighbors know each other and parents don't worry because their kids are playing baseball in the streets. It's the kind of place where homeowners care enough to trim the neat rows of hedges that hug their front porches.

Duluth is the kind of American city most people figure doesn't exist anymore. But it does. And it doesn't take long to discover.

To get a feel for Duluth, you really need to explore it. Take a drive. Don't be afraid to leave the car next to the curb so you can wander on foot and discover for yourself why Duluthians quietly tolerate seven or eight months of winter a year as though there's some secret that makes it all worthwhile.

On a crisp, clear, fall afternoon, head back up the Duluth hillside to that point on Interstate 35 where you were first welcomed by those sparkling diamonds of light.

Roll slowly down the hill. When the road levels off and the Lake Superior Paper Industries paper mill comes into view on the right, look for Grand Avenue. The four-lane road, lined by pine trees and one-story homes, is also Minnesota Highway 23, the original link between Duluth and the Twin Cities, about 150 miles to the south.

Running parallel to the tea-colored St. Louis River, Grand Avenue is home to hiking and biking trails, a zoo and a string of neighborhoods that were once small, independent, industrial townsites.

Probably the most independent of all was Morgan Park.

A familiar sight—freighters passing by the lighthouse at Canal Park.

You'll see a sign for the old company town at a set of traffic lights that always seem to be green. Morgan Park Road leads you under an old railroad bridge and takes you back in time.

This neighborhood is filled with gently curving streets and concrete houses, built comfortably alongside well-kept sidewalks. Built side by side, some of the houses are painted bright shades of yellow, green or blue now. Most are still light brown. And most still look much the

same as they did when U.S. Steel built them for their workers back in 1913. Each still has two front doors, a wide porch and steeply pitched eaves. Driving by, you still half expect to see women in long dresses shaking out rugs.

There was a time when everyone who lived in Morgan Park worked at the steel mill. Whistle blasts from the plant called men to work and announced shift changes. People set their clocks by the noon whistle and told their children to be home before the evening blasts.

The town was named for J.P. Morgan, the financier who helped organize U.S. Steel in the 1800s. The self-sufficient town included a hospital, school and a dormitory for bachelor workers. The company provided a police force, water service, a department store, mail delivery, school and a community club. U.S. Steel also picked up garbage and if you didn't mow your lawn, no problem. They'd do it for you.

And then send a bill.

U.S. Steel's model city received national media attention

when it was first built. And though the city has been a part of Duluth since 1942, it still has the feel of a separate city.

Tucked quietly away from busy Grand Avenue, Morgan Park is a community truly preserved in time.

The best way to explore it is to drive slowly from the Protestant church at one end of the neighborhood to the Catholic church at the other end. Turn past the large gears that mark the entrance to the old steel plant, now a spooky, deserted place.

The quiet road winds through forested lots and forgotten streets where planned-for houses were never built. The road leads under yet another wood and concrete railroad bridge and takes you back to the present day.

Turn onto Grand Avenue and head east, following the signs to Riverside.

Like Morgan Park, this neighborhood was once its own city. And also like Morgan Park, it was built for workers of a nearby industry. This time it was shipbuilding, an industry that flourished during both world wars.

A marina has long since replaced the shipyards, but Riverside is still a tidy community of homes built closely together on streets with names like England Avenue and Union Avenue.

Along one edge of the neighborhood is the Willard Munger Trail. It's eventually supposed to

Those warm, friendly city lights here in north-eastern Minnesota are certain to hold your eyes' attention.

run all the way to Minneapolis. Already, it snakes through the woods on its way to Hinckley, Minnesota.

As you continue toward downtown, turn into the Lake Superior Zoological Gardens, marked by a large sign on the north side of Grand Avenue. Built in the shadow of the city-owned Spirit Mountain Recreation Area ski hill, the zoo has been a Duluth landmark since 1923 when Duluth printer Bert Onsgard rescued a fawn he found wandering through an abandoned logging camp. He took the animal home and somehow managed to convince city leaders to donate land for a zoo.

Within a decade, more than half a million visitors toured a zoo that had become home to more than 400 animals. During the Great Depression of the 1930s, Works Progress Administration (WPA) workers built bridges and outbuildings that are still used today and now give the zoo an old, familiar feel.

A few blocks west of the zoo, the odors of fresh-baked donuts,

the sounds of newsstands and corner bars, and the coziness of small pizza places will call you into West Duluth. It's another neighborhood that's truly a city within the city.

In fact, it had its own borders up until January 1, 1894, when West Duluth was married— literally married—to Duluth.

The city band blared Sousa marches in old Central High School that day as the City Council president lamented the lack of a wedding ring or the presence of bridesmaids. But when the Rev. C.C. Salter paid tribute to the men and women who founded Duluth and praised old-timers for avoiding bigotry, the marriage ceremony was under way. It concluded with those customary words, "Whom God in his kind providence has joined together, let no man put asunder." It was never reported whether anyone kissed anyone else, but at that moment, West Duluth and Duluth were one.

It doesn't take long to get through West Duluth. Before you know it, you'll pass by large, gritty factories, the industry base that once gave Duluth its reputation as a working class town.

Hang a right on 40th Avenue West and head for the waterfront. Down by the ore docks and grain elevators, large ships are being loaded with mountains of coal or taconite. It's a sight that's identifiably Duluth.

7

Above: *A pleasant way to celebrate the dog days.*
Facing page: *Morning spectacle over Lake Superior.* NORMAN A. PETERSON II/UNICORN STOCK PHOTOS

For the best viewing, drive to the other side of the interstate and follow the frontage road to the Duluth, Missabe & Iron Range Railway Co. (DM&IR) ore dock No. 6. Built in 1917, the mammoth dock stretches nearly a half mile into St. Louis Bay. Ore trains rumble across the top of the dock and look like toys as they bring cargo for the 1,000-foot freighters that pull up alongside. The freighters look like miniature replicas.

Climb to the top of the metal and concrete viewing stand on the edge of the DM&IR parking lot and watch as cascades of taconite are poured from the train cars, through chutes in the dock and into the bellies of the giant ships below.

Duluthians proudly boast that their harbor is the world's most inland seaport and is the westernmost terminus of the St. Lawrence Seaway. Half of the port's tonnage is taconite pro-

duced on Minnesota's Iron Range. Most of it is destined for steel mills on the lower Great Lakes where it is turned into cars, ovens and other metal products.

But other mineral exports, including low-sulfur coal from Montana, bentonite, coke and scrap iron, are bound for ports in Europe, Scandinavia and Asia, in addition to American cities.

As the loaded ships pull away from Dock 6, point your car toward the frontage road and make your way back over the interstate. Catch Michigan Street and turn left toward those floodlights that stretch toward the sky and beckon you to a ballgame.

The lights keep watch over Duluth's old, brick baseball stadium and its history of simpler times—warm, lazy evenings at the ballpark—back when Eddie Matthews and Harmon Killebrew ruled the basepaths.

Wade Stadium was built in 1939 and 1940 by Works Progress Administration (WPA) crews who used bricks removed when Grand Avenue was rebuilt.

The stadium was originally called the All-Sports Stadium and was equipped with lights so that Manager Frank Wade and his Duluth Dukes could play night games. When Wade died in 1953, the community insisted that the stadium be named for their coach.

There's been a lot of professional baseball played at the Wade over the years, the kind of baseball that only minor leaguers can play. There have been a few errors committed here, sure, but Duluth has always taken pride in being home to that brand of baseball that comes from the heart and is inspired by a love for the game rather than a big-league paycheck. It's the kind of hard-

working baseball that in a lot of ways reflects the city.

The Northern Baseball League was organized in 1908, with teams in Duluth; Superior, Wisconsin; Minneapolis, Minnesota; Red Wing, Minnesota; Grand Forks, North Dakota; Winona, Minnesota; and Winnipeg, Ontario, Canada.

Duluth fans cheered their Dukes to league pennants in 1909 and 1910. And through the years, they marveled at future big leaguers who started at Wade Stadium and went on to play for the St. Louis Cardinals, the old Cincinnati Red Legs and the Chicago White Sox, all of which owned farm teams in Duluth.

The old Duluth Dukes played their last game at Wade Stadium in 1970, leaving the field to amateurs who played more than 100 games a year.

In 1984, a group of Duluthians calling themselves "Save the Wade" raised money to restore the city stadium.

With the help of Duluth city officials, a new roof was built over the grandstand, lighting was improved and new dugouts were built. In the summer of 1993, a capacity crowd welcomed the Duluth-Superior Dukes back to the Wade, a true testament that Duluthians don't often forget their past.

The Dukes aren't affiliated with a major-league baseball team anymore, but they're still professional, and they still attract as many as two or three thousand fans to their Northern League games.

After a ballgame, take Superior Street east through Duluth's working class West End. The "friendly West End," as it bills itself, is filled with handsome two-story homes, small coffee shops, furniture stores, and thrift shops. Young trees poke through brick

> *Some have speculated the magic lies with the lake.*

sidewalks, welcoming shoppers and visitors to this active neighborhood.

Superior Street will lead you through the West End, past a mountain of black rock known simply as "Point of Rocks" and into downtown, truly the heart of the city.

Downtown Duluth is an active place these days, filled with hurried office workers and shoppers who bustle quickly and warmly inside enclosed "skywalks." Connecting almost all the downtown buildings, you could spend all day visiting the restaurants, bookstores and jewelers

that line the skywalk system.

Or you could take a walk down by the old train depot near 5th Avenue West and Michigan Street. The turreted brick building was built in 1892 and at one time was the largest of the Duluth depots. But those were the days before cars, buses and airplanes.

Today, "The Depot," as it's still affectionately known, is the St. Louis County Heritage and Arts Center. It is home to three museums, exhibition areas, and offices for cultural organizations such as the Duluth Playhouse, the Duluth-Superior Symphony Orchestra, the Duluth Art Institute and the Minnesota Ballet.

Vintage trains still fill the Depot's lower level. A rare collection of engines includes the tiny *Minnetonka*, just 27.5 feet in length, and the mighty *Mallet*, about five times as long. Hop aboard. Pull the whistle. Turn the engine's wheels and pretend you're a conductor.

Or if you want a taste of the real thing, hop a ride with the North Shore Scenic Railroad. Located on the west end of the Depot on that same lower level, it offers hour-and-a-half excursion rides through Duluth's wooded eastern neighborhoods or an all-day trip up the North Shore of Lake Superior to the city of Two Harbors.

From the Depot, hike up the hill along 5th Avenue West. Follow the twinkling white lights that fill the street's ash trees and give

GREG RYAN & SALLY BEYER

JACK RENDULICH

Above: *Tettegouche State Park is a must for tourists.*
Left: *Twilight brings yet another dimension to Superior Street.*

The William Crooks *at The Depot, St. Louis County Heritage and Arts Center.*

Downtown delight.

downtown a nighttime glow. You'll feel the Duluth hillside in your legs as you make your way up. But don't be embarrassed. Everyone breathes hard when they finally reach the lighted, bubbling fountain in the heart of the Civic Center courtyard. Feel free to throw a penny into the water, pull up a wooden bench and relax a bit. Enjoy that unbelievable view of the Duluth-Superior harbor.

The Civic Center is the governmental heart of Duluth, the seat of St. Louis County. Around you are the county courthouse, city hall and the federal building, three majestic buildings complete with pillars and archways and an air of formality.

The St. Louis County Courthouse at center is the largest and most ornate of the three stone structures. It's also the oldest, built in 1911 for $1 million. Chicago architect Daniel Burnham, the father of the "City Beautiful" school of architecture, chose 5th Avenue West and First Street for the courthouse because it was conveniently up the hill from the busy train depot.

Ten stone lion-heads stand guard around the building's large double doors and the wide, marble hallways inside echo with the sounds of hurried feet.

Duluth City Hall at the eastern end of the Civic Center was

Left: *The Bayfront Blues Festival is Duluth's largest outdoor concert event, held each summer in Bayfront Festival Park.*
Below: *Glensheen is alive with the sound of music.*
Bottom: *Wade Stadium was originally called the All-Sports Stadium when it was built in 1939 and 1940 by WPA crews, who used bricks removed when Grand Avenue was rebuilt. Today's Duluth-Superior Dukes of the Northern League have no trouble attracting fans to their baseball games.*

built in 1928, designed by local architect Thomas Shefchik. Portraits of all of Duluth's mayors are displayed on the second floor. And the spacious rotunda is the site of many public ceremonies and home to one of the city's tallest Christmas trees each year. Homemade decorations are cut out and pasted together by the city's schoolchildren and hung from the tree's branches, kind of making it their tree.

The federal building to the west was built two years after City Hall and is easily the least ornate of the three structures. Inside are the offices of federal agencies, including the U.S. Forest Service, and a post office branch.

All three buildings overlook a beautiful courtyard filled with lines of blooming flowers, trimmed shrubs and a graceful, curved brick driveway. It's a great place for downtown workers to take their coffee breaks or eat lunch.

The bricks that cover the walkways here are different from other bricks on downtown sidewalks and streets. These bricks have messages etched into them—names, love notes and dates. The city sold hundreds of them for $25 each when the courtyard was remodeled, ensuring that some Duluthians would forever be immortalized. Even if it is under foot.

Downtown Duluth is a great place to wander. Almost any building offers breathtaking views

They built a fantasy world complete with a Viking ship, turrets, mazes of wobbly walkways, twisting slides— one that comes out of a dragon's head—and swinging tires.

of Lake Superior. As do the quaint, brick streets and avenues that lead you to bakeries, art galleries, bookstores and dozens of small shops.

As you explore, be sure to glance up once in a while. Take note of Duluth's history as it's written on the faces of the older buildings. For example, the original jail is located at 126 E. Superior St., which is now the home of an architectural firm. But "POLICE" is still etched into the brownstone over one of the building's historic archways. It won't take long to discover other nuggets of the past, such as the old *Duluth Herald* building.

Head back to Fifth Avenue West and give your legs a break by walking downhill. Go past the Depot and over the interstate "bridge." Let the playful sounds of

squealing children guide you to Bayfront Festival Park.

The 14-acre, lakefront park is marked by a castle-like playground at one corner and an oversized lemon-colored tent at the opposite end. The tent protects a concert stage from the mist and splashing waves of the nearby Duluth-Superior harbor.

Almost every weekend during the summer, crowds of people flock to the park for shows, ethnic celebrations and other festivals. And since 1989, they've jammed the park for the Bayfront Blues Festival, a two-day outdoor concert that attracts as many as 70,000 people to the waterfront and is easily the region's premier outdoor music event.

But it's that playground over by the parking lot that attracts the most visitors to Bayfront Festival Park.

Most of them are pint sized, sure, but that only seems fair. It was the city's children who designed the playground, collected 1.2 million pennies to pay for it and then got grown-ups to donate wood and nails and help them pound together a child-sized slice of heaven that once existed only in their collective imaginations.

Called Playfront, the 10,000-square-foot playground was built in five days during the summer of 1990 by more than 3,000 volunteers. They gladly took time off from work and other activities, all for the city's children. The mas-

Now a floating museum, the Irvin *was pushed by two tugboats into its present home along the Duluth lakeshore in the summer of 1986.*

sive undertaking was spearheaded and coordinated by the Junior League of Duluth.

With more than a ton of nails and 30,000 feet of donated lumber—six miles worth if laid out end to end—they built a fantasy world complete with a Viking ship, turrets and mazes of wobbly walkways, twisting slides and swinging tires. There's even a circular slide that comes out of a dragon's head.

Across the street from Playfront is northeastern Minnesota's hub of sports, culture and the arts. Folks here call the arena-auditorium complex "the deck" for the acronym DECC, which stands for Duluth Entertainment Convention Center. From its opening in 1966 until its expansion in 1990, it was called the Duluth Arena-Auditorium Complex.

If you're lucky, the Duluth-Superior Symphony Orchestra will be performing in the auditorium or perhaps a touring Broadway show or rock band will be on stage in the arena.

The DECC has hosted concerts ranging from Barry Manilow to Randy Travis to Metallica, and shows featuring everything from dogs to boats to interior decorating.

Each winter, the Duluth-based Minnesota Ballet performs "The Nutcracker." The DECC is also home to some of the best college hockey in the nation. The University of Minnesota-Duluth Bulldogs pack the house with fans hungry to see stars like Derek Plante, Brett Hull, Jim Johnson, Norm Maciver and Tom Kurvers, all of whom have gone on to play in the NHL.

The Bulldogs best season was 1984 when they played what is now considered the greatest game in Bulldog history—and probably the greatest game in NCAA tournament history. That year, the Bulldogs skated against Bowling Green for the national championship in Lake Placid, New York, losing after four heartbreaking overtimes, 5-4.

Winter-happy Duluthians don't just love hockey, though. Curling is the game most often played in the DECC's Pioneer Hall. It's a sport played in Duluth since 1891 when the first curling club was organized. Within a few years, the club was considered one of the country's finest. One of the club's first rinks, at 1330 London Road, had 12 sheets of curling ice, the most under one roof anywhere in the United States at the time.

The elegant and spacious DECC convention center that opened in 1990 was built to look a little like a lake vessel. The center features luxurious and highly versatile meeting rooms, a columnless

The throaty Wuuuuuum...Wuuum call of an ore carrier mixes with the shrill cries of gulls overhead.

ballroom and a bubbling fountain that greets visitors to the atrium. There's even a room in the convention center named for the well-known Lake Superior shipwreck of the *Edmund Fitzgerald*, the 730-foot ore carrier that went down on November 10, 1975. Ironically but intentionally, it's located directly below the Lake Superior Room.

One of the grandest of all Great Lakes vessels was the *William A. Irvin*. You'll see the brick-red freighter docked near the DECC. Long yellow stairways reach to shore and welcome you aboard.

Now a floating museum, the *Irvin* was pushed by two tugboats into its present home along the Duluth lakeshore in the summer of 1986. It's strictly a tourist attraction now, but in its active days, the ship was both a workhorse and a showpiece.

Built in 1938, the Irvin was the first Great Lakes vessel launched after the Great Depression devastated the lakes shipping industry. It was U.S. Steel's flagship until 1972 and often welcomed VIPs into its rich mahogany guest quarters. Its elegance earned the *Irvin* the nickname "the pride of the silver stackers," referring to the color of the black-banded smokestacks that were distinctive of U.S. Steel's fleet.

Guests feasted on lobster dinners and stayed in plush quarters. They played shuffleboard between the rock-red hatches on deck that covered the ship's ore-filled, taconite-filled or coal-filled holds. Some guests drove golf balls from the hatchtops to the bottom of the lake, or they tried to tightrope-walk their way down hatchcrane rails that ran the length of the spotless red deck. A few even flew kites from the stern.

The 610-foot *Irvin* became obsolete during the 1970s when a new breed of thousand-foot ships was produced. The new freighters carried more cargo, moved faster and required smaller crews.

The *Irvin* was retired in 1978 and was nearly forgotten in a Twin Ports shipyard for eight years. The once-proud boat was saved from the scrap yard when the State Convention Board bought it for $110,000 and then spent another $210,000 to refurbish it and turn it into an attractive and important part of the Duluth lakeshore.

Take a guided tour, then head for the bright blue pedestrian bridge just beyond the *Irvin*'s stern. Marked by the bronze statues (now oxidized green) of dancing fish, the bridge—when it's not up to allow charter fishing boats to pass—leads across the *Irvin*'s slip and into Canal Park, one of Minnesota's most-famous and best-known travel destinations.

The once dilapidated warehouse district was home to junk yards and gritty factories. It was little more than a seedy hangout where sailors came to drink.

But a multimillion dollar face-lift during the 1980s turned Canal Park into the picturesque mecca it is today. Lined by quaint stores, cafes, bakeries and gift shops, it's a wanderers' heaven.

The thick aroma of espresso wafts deliciously from small coffee shops as the throaty *Wuuuuuuum... Wuuum-wuuum* call of an ore carrier mixes with the shrill cries of gulls overhead.

You can get almost anything in Canal Park, from jelly beans to

Vietnamese food to Christmas lights in the shape of fish. In one restaurant, you can even watch live indoor basketball games as you eat pizza.

But the thing that draws people to Canal Park more than anything else is the great Aerial Lift Bridge, Duluth's most famous, most photographed and most talked about landmark.

The towering, steel-beamed superstructure glows spectacularly at night under the shower of high-powered floodlights. It's "a maze of steel beams and girders like an Erector set, with a small, window-lined house perched above where the bridge operators work," longtime Duluthian Laurie Hertzel wrote in her 1993 book *Boomtown Landmarks*.

The bridge was built in 1905, more than 30 years after a canal was dug through Minnesota Point to open the Duluth harbor to shipping traffic.

In the three decades before the bridge was built, the people who lived on the Point crossed the canal any way they could. In the winter, they walked slowly and carefully over the unpredictable ice. And in the summer, they took 10¢ ferries. For a short time prior to the turn of the 20th century, a rope walkway spanned the canal. It was so wobbly, though, that people often had to crawl across it.

A bridge was needed, one that was tall enough for masted vessels and low enough for people. A bridge

like the one that spanned the Seine River in Rouen, France.

Modeled after the French bridge, Duluth's version was originally known as the Aerial Ferry Bridge. Rather than having a ground-level roadway span that lifted whenever a boat wanted to pass under, this bridge featured a gondola that hung from cables and could carry up to six automobiles. Cars and pedestrians boarded at one side and then were moved slowly to the other side.

In 1930, as more and more people owned cars, however, the bridge became inadequate and had to be remodeled. Its side towers were raised and reinforced, and the gondola was replaced with a rising road deck that tourists and locals still find fascinating.

On a warm summer evening, stand underneath the bridge. Close your eyes and listen. Let the laughter of children, the excited voices of Duluth visitors, the slapping of waves against the cement piers, and the high-pitched *cawww-cawww* cries of gulls wash over you.

It's a magical, joyous and peaceful place.

Until the bell sounds.

That's an unspoken signal for everyone to rush past you to the edge of the cement piers. Out in the lake, a Great Lakes freighter is steaming slowly past the Duluth skyline on its way to the harbor entry. The bell continues to ring as the bridge span slowly lifts. It's a spectacular sight as it rises above you

The Aerial Lift Bridge, which originally featured a gondola that was filled with people and vehicles and then moved across the canal, has always provided photo opportunities.

120 feet. Crane your neck to see the massive cables, as thick as your forearm, and the 970-ton counterweights as they offset the weight of the rising deck.

The monstrous ship sails quietly, almost silently, between the two lighthouses that mark the canal's opening. Then with a sound like a hundred fog horns, the ship's skipper signals the bridge. *Wuuuuuuum...Wuuum-wuuum!* With a slightly higher-pitched horn of its own, the bridge responds: *Wooooooom... Wooom-wooom!*

In homes on the Duluth hillside, residents ignore the TV long enough to push aside their drapes and welcome the boat to town. On the piers, startled onlookers giggle at the way they jumped when the horns blasted and then wave to the deckhands and bearded seamen. The sailors often wave back, enjoying the spectacle as much as the people on shore.

After the bridge drops back to its original position, wander into the Marine Museum. Climb into its turn-of-the-century pilot house, stand behind the ship's wheel and gaze across Lake Superior. With a child's imagination, pretend you're the one who just maneuvered that giant vessel into the harbor.

The romance and adventure of shipping attract as many as 6,000 people a day to the Canal Park Visitors Center and Marine Museum, which is run by the U.S. Army Corps of Engineers.

Exhibits include models of ore docks, videos about Great Lakes shipping, artifacts from sunken ships, and full-size cabin replicas with mannequins that "talk" to you and tell you about life on board.

Next, drive across the Aerial Lift Bridge to explore Minnesota

JACK RENDULICH

Above: *Can there possibly be a better place to watch the sunrise?*
Facing page: *A special look at Minnesota Point.*

Point. It's Duluth's most unusual neighborhood and quite possibly the coldest place during a Minnesota summer. Regardless, the Point's beaches are full on warm days.

The Point—the longest freshwater sandbar in the world—is wide enough in most places for only one long, two-lane street and the houses that grace either side. So if you get stuck behind a slow motorist, sit back and enjoy the drive.

Enjoy the old bungalows and giant beach houses that fill the Point. Almost all the homes are on the water—either on Lake Superior or the Duluth harbor. And almost all have large windows and even larger lake-view decks.

The Point is home to the U.S. Coast Guard and its buoy tender, *Sundew*. The 50-year-old ship breaks ice in the spring and fall to keep the shipping season open as long as possible.

The Point is also home to the Duluth Rowing Club, a group not unlike the curling club in the way it once put Duluth in the national sporting spotlight.

Rowing crested at a glorious level between 1911 and 1923 when Duluth teams won 20 national championships. Its teams were so good, in fact, that some Eastern newspapers suggested the city was using professionals.

Competitive rowing has its earliest roots in Duluth in 1871 when athletes reportedly raced using birch-bark canoes. The city still has teams in national and Midwestern rowing circles, but their success is only marginal compared to the heyday of the sport.

When you reach the softball fields and sand pit volleyball courts at the end of the Point, turn around and head back toward Canal Park.

If you get stuck behind a long line of cars in front of the ship canal, consider yourself "bridged." Waiting in your car for a ship to pass under the Aerial Lift Bridge is an inconvenience Point residents live with much of the year. It's a lot like waiting for a train to pass, only there's a little more romance and the wait is often longer when waiting on a ship. When you do finally cross listen to the way your car's rubber tires sound like fighter jets in those old World War II movies as they press against the bridge's metal surface. On the other side, turn right toward the rocky lakeshore.

Give yourself the time to stroll leisurely along the wooden boardwalk that gently hugs the corner of Lake Superior and connects downtown Duluth to the lakefront. The three-mile path leads you past metal interpretive signs that explain some of Duluth's history, past Lake Place Park, which was built on top of the interstate to give downtown workers a link to the lake, past the Vietnam War Memorial, the old Fitger's Brewery, and finally past Leif Erikson Park, where you can see the replica of an old Viking ship.

On a blacktop path that runs parallel to the boardwalk, skaters and bikers zip by. Like the boardwalk, the blacktop path weaves its way around small trees, blooming flower beds, hidden beaches and wooden park benches.

It also takes you to several metal and concrete stairways that lead into downtown. Climb up the one near Fitger's, a low-slung brick building marked by a tall, brick smokestack.

Inside, posh gift shops line meandering hallways in the old brewery. It's a browser's paradise. The shops connect a luxury hotel and a couple of restaurants. A patio behind the building is filled with lake watchers on almost any summer evening.

Fitger's hasn't always been an upscale shopping center, however.

It was a struggling brewery in a struggling young town when it first opened in 1881 with three hard-working employees.

August Fitger, who learned the art of brewing in his homeland Germany, bought half interest in the brewery in 1883, fulfilling his dream to own a brewery in America. He expanded the operation and used his own recipes. He modernized and streamlined the brewery, and by 1910 it was one of the largest and most up-to-date in Minnesota.

In its prime, Fitger's employed 250 people and turned out more than 150,000 barrels of beer a year.

Fitger's shut its doors in 1972 and for years the building

sat abandoned, the vats empty, the smokestack dormant. A chain link fence kept out the curious.

The classy building was eventually renovated and reopened. Refreshingly, it still has the feel of an old brewery, and you can still buy Fitger's Beer inside.

Enjoy one. Or two.

If beer's not your thing, though, there's a tiny, easy-to-miss brick structure next door that serves the best milkshakes in town. Possibly the best in Minnesota. Folks in Duluth mark the passage of winter as the day the Portland Malt Shoppe opens.

Built as it is, so precariously close to the stone retaining wall that overlooks the big lake, it's hard to believe the one-room building was once a gas station—one of Duluth's earliest.

Sip your shake or munch on the wafer cookie they stick into the thick, creamy ice cream, and wander down the path that leads along that rocky "cliff." A large, stately, mansion-like building filled with leaded glass windows, high ceilings and Tudor trim is almost certain to catch your eye on the other side of busy Superior Street.

It's the Kitchi Gammi Club, a symbol of wealth and power in Duluth. The kind of wealth that built this city. The kind of power that elevated it and set it apart from other frontier fur trading posts.

The Kitch, as it's known, is a very exclusive, somewhat mysterious place. Most Duluthians have

never seen its chestnut-paneled walls or walked across its plush, red carpeting. They figure something important is going on inside—it's just that kind of place.

At least 83 Great Lakes ships have been named for Kitchi Gammi Club members as the private club has been home away from home for mining and railroad barons for more than a century. To this day, it boasts a membership list that reads like a Who's Who in Duluth.

And although business meetings are still held in the Kitch's eight dining rooms, the days are gone when the city's future was

> *Drive through the Duluth tunnels that were built, in part, to protect the highway from freezing lake mist.*

decided within the walls of Minnesota's first private men's club.

Still, visiting executives are often wined and dined at the Kitchi Gammi, meaning "great water," the Chippewa name for Lake Superior.

Stroll back down Superior Street as it leads through an often

forgotten section of downtown, that section east of Lake Avenue that used to be the heart of the city. Hang a left on Lake Avenue and walk toward the waterfront, past the clock tower and back into Canal Park to get your car.

You'll want to catch the interstate next and drive east to explore Duluth's traditionally white-collar eastern neighborhoods. This is the side of town where mining barons, lumber kings, shipbuilders and high-powered attorneys built their spacious and awesome mansions, each with views of Lake Superior. To a lesser degree, eastern Duluth is still considered home to the city's rich and influential.

Drive through the Duluth tunnels that were built, in part, to protect the highway from freezing lake mist, and head past a string of hotels that fill up on almost any weekend because of their easy access to the freeway and breathtaking views of Lake Superior. Drive until Interstate 35 ends at 26th Avenue East. The southern terminus of the freeway is in Laredo, Texas, on the Mexican border.

Turn right for a self-guided tour of the lakefront's stately mansions, most built during the late 1800s and early 1900s. Notice the turrets, stained glass windows, rolling green lawns, tennis courts, fountains, and huge gardens. These are wooded properties rimmed with brick walls and protected by stone lions that guard front gates. They're the

BOB FIRTH

Left: *Glensheen, built in 1905, was the home of mining and lumber king Chester A. Congdon. Today, the mansion is open for public tours.*
Below: *A great day for celebrating the setting.*

Facing page, top: *"...we all dwell in a house of one room—the world with the firmament for its roof—and are sailing the celestial spaces without leaving any track."*
—John Muir
Bottom: *Lake Superior Museum at the entrance to the Duluth-Superior Harbor.*

JACK RENDULICH

former homes of people such as author Sinclair Lewis, who wrote *Main Street*, *Babbitt* and other great American novels; or Chester A. Congdon, a mining and lumber king who made a fortune on the Minnesota Iron Range.

In 1905, Congdon decided to build his family's home on a 7.5-acre lot overlooking the point where Tischer Creek pours into Lake Superior.

Within three years, he created Glensheen, as it came to be known, a symbol of elaborate elegance and Victorian luxury in a city that was just emerging from its rugged, wild and unsettled frontier days.

Congdon filled the 39-room home with Oriental rugs; rich oak paneling; textured English leather ceilings; wall coverings of damask made from goat's hair; 15 fireplaces, one faced with red marble from Algeria; and mahogany furniture with upholstery that was hand woven in Germany.

Nothing was too good for his family's home.

Today, the mansion is still a shrine to affluence. It's been open for public tours since 1979. Take a walk through. It's a rare chance to see how the other half lived.

But remember that many of the 100,000 or so visitors who tour the Glensheen each year don't come just to look at the silver light fixtures or the green-tiled breakfast room. The mansion is also the site of Duluth's most famous double murder, a crime that remains one of Minnesota's most notorious whodunits.

On the night of June 27, 1977, Roger Caldwell threw a heavy object through a window in the billiard room and broke into the mansion. He then felt his way around the billiard table and up the stairs. By his own account, he beat a night nurse to death with a candlestick and then smothered her patient, 83-year-old Elisabeth Congdon, the last remaining child of Chester Congdon, and heiress to his fortune. Caldwell, who was Elisabeth Congdon's son-in-law, was convicted of the murders long after the home was open to the public. His wife, Marjorie, was acquitted.

There's no mention of the murders during the guided tours, which is just as well. It'd be a shame to preoccupy yourself with gruesome details and miss the plush details of a pampered life in a bygone era.

Continue driving east on London Road. Catch glimpses of Lake Superior as it sparkles through the trees that shade the giant houses.

Slow down when you see the old fish hatchery on the lake side of the road. A white gingerbread-house–like building, the hatchery was the first artificial spawning operation on Lake Superior. The building is now on the National Register of Historic Places.

Alongside the hatchery, the Lester River bubbles into Lake Superior, creating a white foam that floats on top of the water. Anglers dressed in waders lob spoons or spawn sacks into the icy waters here, hoping for a chinook or steelhead.

Wind your way up along the rocky banks of the Lester to Superior Street. Follow the green and white "Skyline Parkway" signs to the top of the Duluth hillside, where you'll find Hawk Ridge and other breathtaking vistas.

Below Hawk Ridge, neat lines of rooftops crisscross the wooded hillside. The middle- and upper middle-class homes here in the Lester Park and Lakeside neighborhoods stretch to the shores of Lake Superior, its own blueness stretching away from you until it meets the blue of the sky on the horizon.

Looking out from Hawk Ridge, it's nearly possible to comprehend the awesome size of Lake Superior, the biggest body of fresh water in the world. It's 380 miles long, 160 miles across and has a maximum depth of 1,300 feet.

Scientists tell us that the lake was left in the wake of a receding glacier 10,000 years ago. In fact, the original shoreline of the glacial lake was supposedly up near Skyline Drive and Hawk Ridge, some 400 feet above the lake's present shores.

Lake Superior is so big that the states of Massachusetts, Connecticut, Vermont and New Hampshire could fit within its 32,483 square miles and inside its 2,796 miles of shoreline.

It's a marvel to look at.

But there's more to see from Hawk Ridge than the great lake.

On bright fall afternoons when the winds are blowing out of the west or northwest, bird lovers from across the Midwest crowd onto Hawk Ridge, binoculars in hand, to watch anywhere from 30,000 to 75,000 migrating hawks on their journey to southern states, Mexico, Central America and South America.

The sharp-shinned hawks are joined by barred owls, peregrine falcons, bald eagles, and other birds from distant points north. They come from the far corners of northeastern Minnesota, from Manitoba and northeast Ontario. Some even make the trip from high arctic regions. Not wanting to cross the massive expanse of Lake Superior, the birds fly close to the crest of the hillside as they pass Duluth.

Hundreds of die-hard birders and casual bird-watchers come too. To watch, to count and to marvel at the raptors during the annual Hawk Ridge Weekends.

Drive east along Skyline Parkway, a lazy, romantic two-lane road built sometimes frighteningly too close to the crest of the Duluth hillside. Trees and brush grow wild along the roadside and infringe little on the spectacular sight of Duluth, the lake and northwestern Wisconsin on the other side of the water as they unfold before you.

Park Point, the Duluth ship canal and the East Hillside hospital district come into view before you pass the sprawling University of Minnesota-Duluth campus. All of its buildings are connected by corridors and walkways so that students don't have to bear the elements during harsh Duluth winters. Duluth's finest museum, the Tweed Museum of Art, has its home at the university.

Turn off Skyline when you reach Chester Bowl, a park filled with nature trails, the sparkling Chester Creek, playgrounds and trees. Like so many of Duluth's parks and neighborhoods, Chester Bowl has that out-in-the-middle-of-the-woods feel despite being only a couple of miles from downtown.

But it hasn't always been a quiet place. It was once home to large ski jumping events back when Duluth was known as the "Ski Jumping Capital of the United States."

The Duluth Ski Club was first organized in November of 1905. A year later, the club's Ole Feiring won the national championship. He repeated in 1907 with a leap of 112 feet, 30 feet longer than the previous world record.

In 1924, the club built the largest steel slide in the world. And in 1932, Carl Holstrom made the U.S. Olympic team. Also during this era, George Kotlarek held the national championship in four classes on different occasions. For decades,

the Chester Park Ski Club trained boys in ski jumping, consistently turning out competitors for national and Olympic teams.

Two jumps are all that remain in Chester Bowl to remind Duluthians of a proud era now past.

West of the park, Skyline winds its way peacefully through the woods and past modest, two-story homes. Most have wide front porches that hold snuggling couples on warm summer evenings. Through the trees, downtown Duluth glistens under a warm sun as Skyline Parkway takes you above the heart of the city. Slow down. Toe the road's gritty edge and just look.

Let the scenic drive lead you to Enger Tower for what is arguably the best view in the city.

The stone tower is a true Duluth landmark and looks a lot like the remains of an ancient lookout, though it's really not that old. The octagonal structure was built in 1939 as a tribute to Bert Enger, a self-made success who moved to Duluth from Norway.

"From common laborer to merchant prince," a bronze plaque inside the tower proclaims about Enger, "he demonstrated in his own life that America is a land of opportunity for the immigrant and that her civilization is enriched by his citizenship."

Let a stone path lead you past lush gardens and brilliant flower beds to the tower. Walk up its winding stone staircase. It's

cool and a little dark inside, and once you reach the top, it's always windy. But the view is worth any chill.

On the hillside behind you, golfers lift towering shots over perfect blue ponds. Homeowners spray water onto thick lawns. And dogs lead owners across quiet, tree-lined boulevards.

The city stretches out in front of you much the way it did when you first crested the Duluth hillside back on Interstate 35.

Fishing boats bob playfully in the St. Louis River as loaded ore carriers, riding low in the water,

glide silently past the grain elevators and factories that freckle the lakeshore. The Aerial Lift Bridge rises, "bridging" a whole line of motorists on either side. Visitors in Canal Park toss popcorn into the air to gulls that squeal overhead.

It's almost time to send the ship on its way, to wish the sailors a safe voyage until they return again. And they will. They always return to Duluth.

Drink it in. From your perch high above the city, let the minutes pass. Relax. Let the city wash over you and take you in.

It's the kind of place where

life is slow, after all, where crime rates are low and where neighbors are always willing to lend a helping hand.

It's the kind of city where you can take in a ballgame or a concert or a play and then see a deer or moose run across the road as you drive home. Duluth is a regional hub for entertainment, medicine and shopping. But from up here, from on top of Enger Tower, you get the feeling the city is still part wilderness, that it somehow has held onto its frontier roots, its rugged reputation.

And its magic.

PHYLLIS KEDL/UNICORN STOCK PHOTOS

Above: *Northeastern Minnesota's hub of sports, culture and the arts—the Duluth Entertainment Convention Center (DECC).*
Left: *A fish out of water.*
Below: *It's always impressive to watch an ore boat come into the channel.*

Facing page: *A walker's paradise, but there are other ways to go.*

RICHARD HAMILTON SMITH

29

From Fur Trading to Tourism

A smattering of mostly modest homes lines the shores of the St. Louis River at the point where Duluth has its earliest roots.

On two playgrounds, children dribble basketballs and swing on tires. At the boat launch, anglers motor from shore in search of walleye. From a bridge that spans the river, you can watch other anglers cast nightcrawlers from shore, see busy campers pile wood together for an evening fire, or wait until nightfall and then watch the green and blue hues of the northern lights as they dance across the sky.

It's Duluth's Fond du Lac neighborhood, located only 14 miles west of a bustling downtown and busy Great Lakes port. But out here where there's still just the river and its high, jagged bluffs, it's still possible to see what once was. In the white pines and maples that line the river, it's possible for our less cynical selves to imagine the fur trading posts that once lined the shores, or the tour boats that chugged up the river during the city's heyday, or the Indians who first made their home at the western tip of Lake Superior.

It was here where French explorer Daniel Greysolon, Sieur du Lhut came in the autumn of 1679 to arrange a truce between warring Indian nations.

At age 40, du Lhut, or Duluth, was an adventurer who already had a reputation as a statesman and visionary. When he was young, he joined the military almost solely because it offered prestige and action at a time when France was often at war with other European nations. He served with distinction, but soon after he turned 30 his hunger for adventure led him to the New World and the city of Quebec. There, he joined his brother and other relatives who had already settled.

In less than a decade he was on the move again. Some say he left Quebec because of a soured romance with the daughter of a prominent local family. But Duluth insisted he simply yearned to explore farther inland.

Traveling with three Indians and seven Frenchmen, Duluth set out for the land of the Dakota Indians, who lived at the western tip of Lake Superior. He had heard the area was swarming with beaver, and was eager to begin trading. But first he needed to make peace between the Dakota and their enemy, the Ojibwe.

He landed on the beaches of what is today Minnesota Point, a peninsula of land that attracts sun worshippers and through which ore carriers and other ships enter the Duluth harbor. He traveled on to Fond du Lac, where the heads of the nations had gathered.

"They all did come," Duluth wrote about the event. "I had the good fortune of gaining their esteem and friendship; and so that peace among them would last longer, I thought I could not cement it better than by arranging reciprocal marriages between nations....The following winter, I had them get together in the woods where I was staying so that they could hunt and feast together and thus establish closer bonds of friendship."

The Dakota and Ojibwe weren't the first people to call the western tip of Lake Superior home, of course. For more than 10,000 years, the area was home to several American Indian nations.

First came the Paleo-Indian cultures who lived in small groups, wore animal skins and hunted deer, elk and caribou. The "Old Copper" cultures came next and were the first in the Americas known to hunt with spear points and knives and fish with metal hooks. Old Copper and other Eastern Archaic peoples hunted both large and small animals, and grew their own vegetables. Woodland cultures inhabited the area around the time that Christ was born. They're best known for their pottery, burial mounds, and annual harvests of wild rice, a crop still harvested and sold by Indians today.

The Dakota Indians occupied much of the area when Duluth and other French explorers arrived. Historian Theodore C. Blegen called the Dakota a wise people who cooked with fire and made pottery. They were also gifted hunters who enjoyed large feasts and loved to play games.

Soon after the French explorers initiated fur trading with the Indians, the Dakota left the area. Non-Dakota history suggests they were driven from their land by the Ojibwe Indians, who with their steel knives, muskets and gun powder, simply overpowered the Dakota. But while Dakota historians concede there was friction between the nations, they insist their people were simply attracted by the Great Plains. The Ojibwe were soon the dominant tribe in Northern Minnesota and still make up much of Duluth's American Indian population.

The history of the Ojibwe is steeped in legend. They were a family-oriented people who held nature sacred. When a hunter stalked a deer, he did so with respect for the animal as the giver of meat and as a holy and valued being. The Ojibwe also recognized the earth as a life-giving storehouse that needed to be cared for—proving that the American Indian was the land's first real caretaker.

The Ojibwe lived along the shores of a great salt water sea to the east before moving to the western Great Lakes under pressure from the Iroquois. They scattered to the north and east, first settling along the shores of Lake Michigan and then Lake Superior. By the time Duluth arrived, they had settled a large village called La Pointe (today, Wisconsin) on Madeline Island, one of Lake Superior's famous Apostle Islands. Duluth spent the winter of 1678-79 with the Ojibwe there, firmly establishing French-Indian trade before his history-making trip to Minnesota Point.

The peace agreement he arranged between the Indian nations was weak at best, but it

Daniel Greysolon, Sieur du Lhut.

opened the area to trade. The Ojibwe served as middlemen between the French and Dakota. The area flourished and populations swelled. It was considered "the golden age of the Ojibwe."

The first fur trading post may have been established as early as 1692 when it is believed that the Hudson's Bay Company, the first great fur trading enterprise, held a small post at Fond du Lac. The main trading center was about 150 miles northeast along Lake Superior's North Shore at a place still known today as Grand Portage. But Fond du Lac was still a busy place, for it was through here that explorers traveled on their way to inland waterways—the rivers, streams and lakes that eventually led explorers to the Mississippi River, and as far West as the Rockies.

It was a century before another trading post operated in Fond du Lac. In 1792, French fur trader Jean Baptiste Cadotte of the North West Company, built a wood picket fort on what is now the Wisconsin side of the St. Louis River. The fort was destroyed by fire in 1800. But less than ten years later, the German-born John Jacob Astor built a trading post on the Minnesota side of the river. The Fond du Lac post was operated by Astor's newly formed American Fur Company, which quickly proved to be a bust as the Indians continued trading with longtime French and English partners.

But Astor didn't give up. He convinced the United States Congress to pass a law barring foreigners from trading in American territory. It was a law that guaranteed him a monopoly on the fur markets. A new American Fur Company, much bigger than the original, was formed in 1816-17. For the next three decades, the post was an island of "civilization" for the Europeans in an otherwise Great Lakes wilderness.

The fur company fell on hard times by 1839. Fashionable Europeans started wearing silk hats rather than ones made from beaver pelts. And while fish from the river and lake were still plenti-

Ojibwe dancer.

The great hall and voyageur's canoe at Grand Portage National Monument, a popular destination of tourists traveling Minnesota Highway 61 as it winds 147 miles from Duluth to the Canadian border at Pigeon River.

ful, the struggling economy meant fewer fish were sold.

Enter copper mining. Tales of valuable reserves had been whispered almost since the time the French came. Now, with hard times, the rumors grew louder. In 1852, the federal government paid for the first land survey. An 1854 treaty with the Indians was followed by a land rush for the choicest parcels of land. Settlers flocked to the western end of Lake Superior in search of the valuable mineral. A treaty with the Indians opened the wilderness to explorers who dreamt of gold and the mineral that would someday prove to be a boon for northeastern Minnesota: iron ore.

Meanwhile, out East, channels and locks were being carved through narrow Great Lakes passageways, allowing large, deepdraft ships to sail into Lake Superior for the first time. Promoters of Duluth predicted the area would surpass Chicago as the focal point for trade between established Eastern cities and the settlers on the Western frontier.

The first road was built, connecting the Lake Superior region to the Twin Cities. Unfortunately, it was "the worst road I have ever experienced," one pioneer wrote. "Much of the way it was mud above our knees."

But it was a start.

Both sides of the St. Louis River flourished. Eleven small towns sprang up around Fond du

> *In those early days we were all neighbors from Beaver Bay down the North Shore to Fond du Lac and over into Superior.*

Lac and Minnesota Point. And Duluth had its roots.

The new communities swelled with immigrants who marveled at cool summer breezes and set down roots in a place that just somehow felt like home. Sawmills buzzed along the St. Louis River and warehouses near the river's mouth quickly filled with food and supplies. A new lighthouse welcomed sailors from eastern ports.

Long, cold winters proved just how isolated the frontier communities were, however. Supplies grew thin as Duluthians learned early on to take storms in stride and to grow tough with the weather. The first ships of spring sailed to Duluth shortly after the ice went out and were always welcomed with cheers from shore.

By 1857, copper resources proved sparse, and timber harvesting quickly became the area's top livelihood.

But a money crisis that

swept the nation that year also affected the tip of the lake. Mineral magnates, timber barons and merchants cut their losses and fled for larger cities back East. Almost three-fourths of the Duluth-area pioneers also left, hoping for better times elsewhere. Lake steamers carried reluctant people away from their homes and the military road to the Twin Cities was crowded with southbound travelers. Those who didn't leave lived on fish and potatoes and banded together to weather the hard times.

"In those early days we were all neighbors from Beaver Bay down the North Shore to Fond du Lac and over into Superior," wrote Alfred Merritt, one of the hearty souls who stuck it out. "One cannot write about just one side of the state line for in sickness and in joy there was no state line."

Neighbor helping neighbor, community helping community. It's a long tradition Northlanders carry on today.

Prosperity returned in the late 1860s when Duluth officials, including financier Jay Cooke, convinced the Lake Superior and Mississippi Railroad to build an extension from St. Paul to Duluth. The rail line would open iron mining north and west of Lake Superior and Duluth would soon become a railroad town—Jay Cooke's town.

"The lifeless corpse of

Duluth...touched by the wand of Jay Cooke, sprang full-armed from the tomb," state Representative James J. Egan, wrote at the time. "[We] won the good fight and henceforth the sun of prosperity gilded the lake and your bluffs echoed and reechoed back the glad acclaim: Minnesota has triumphed!"

Only 14 families were there to celebrate New Year's Day in 1869. But by the Fourth of July, 3,500 people—with more on the way—celebrated the nation's independence in what was becoming a boom town.

The city's first newspaper was published that year when the editor of the *St. Paul Minnesotian* lugged his presses and typesetting equipment to an abandoned barn near the heart of what is still downtown. On April 24, the first edition of the weekly *Duluth Minnesotian* hit the newsstands.

Sawmills continued to thrive up and down the North Shore. A brewery was built. And all along the mud and gravel of Superior Street, Duluthians grabbed up prime downtown lots. They cleared timber and brush from the hillside and nailed together homes and small businesses.

In November, the first telegraph linked Duluth to the world. As Duluth journalist and historian Glenn Sandvik wrote in 1983, "Duluth was overcoming its isolation."

Duluth never quite lived up to predictions of being the next Pittsburgh or Chicago. But in 1907, Duluth's harbor did surpass New York City in gross tonnage handled, making it the leading port in the United States. Indeed, it was shipping that really put Duluth on the map.

The first vessels to call on the Duluth port often meant the difference between life and death as supplies were piled into warehouses for the long, hard winters. But many other ships carried food, clothing and other goods destined for Western states as Duluth continued to be an important bridge between Eastern culture and the Western frontier.

By the early 1900s, Duluth boasted ten newspapers and six banks. Hardware stores, grocery stores, blast furnaces and other small industries freckled its hillside. The first skyscraper, the 11-story Torrey Building, which is still part of the city's skyline, was already a decade old. Schools, theaters, and hotels buzzed with the city's elite. And tourists discovered Duluth's beauty, relaxed pace and cool summers.

Many flocked to town to ride the famous Incline Railway. Originally built by housing developers, the elevated train took tourists and Duluthians alike to the top of the hill that overlooks downtown and Lake Superior. A large wooden pavilion near the upper station was Duluth's cultural and entertainment center. With its dining halls, dancing halls and 1,600-seat auditorium, the pavilion hopped each weekend night. It was destroyed by fire in 1901; the railway itself was torn down and sold for scrap in 1939.

Big-time industry came to Duluth in 1907 when U.S Steel announced it would build a $5 million to $6 million steel plant in the western end of town. It was eight years before steel rolled out of the plant, but predictions were renewed that Duluth would swell to 200,000 or 300,000 people.

A company town named Morgan Park was built alongside the steel plant. Homes made of poured concrete, cinder blocks, and timbers lined wide, well-paved streets. The company discreetly buried sewer, water, and electrical utilities and filled the community with the company's offices, a modern school, community club, and stores. Two churches, one Protestant and one Catholic, still mark either end of Morgan Park.

With U.S. Steel, a cement plant, wire mills, nail mill and other industries in town and a thriving iron ore industry to the north, Duluth helped win both World War I and World War II. Duluthians' most visible contribution was shipbuilding. In 1916, a shipyard along the St. Louis River produced eight vessels at a time. Houses for the workers were built, as were stores, a small hospital and a theater. Riverside quickly became the Morgan Park of Duluth's shipbuilding industry. In all, Duluth and Superior ship-

Above: *Cityscape with lake.*
Facing page: *Basking in the gold of Minnesota's glorious aspens.*

JACK RENDULICH

The pavilion at the top of the Incline Railway was a social gathering place; in fact, it was the *place during Duluth's early years.*

yards produced 103 vessels for the World War I effort.

During World War II, shipyards in Duluth and Superior produced 191 more vessels in seven shipyards that sprang up within a year of the attack on Pearl Harbor. Lifelong Duluthian Bernie Pfeffer, now 80, remembers having to stuff his ears full of cotton to deaden the constant clanging of cranes and hammering of steel.

"It would ring all over the ship," said Pfeffer, an electrician

called with thousands of other Twin Ports men and women to build ships, something many had never done before.

"It's a whole different ball game between home wiring and commercial wiring," he said. "I learned a lot. It was a very rewarding experience. Everybody was really putting out. People had pride in their work. They were doing it for their country."

Duluth's war effort included mostly smaller support ships, while

bigger East Coast shipyards built the Navy's major warships. The support ships included net tenders, which spread nets across harbor entries to keep out enemy submarines; tankers that delivered fresh water to warships; and buoy tenders that marked shipping lanes and kept Great Lakes ports open during the winter so new ships could be launched and delivered. Some of the yards also built coastal freighters and escort warships to protect convoys. The yards operated 24 hours a day, often in bitter cold.

Duluth continued to grow and prosper after the war, riding the wave of a thriving, bustling port. In 1960, the city's population peaked at 106,884 and the future looked bright.

But in 1971, as American industries started moving to Mexico and Japan, U.S. Steel closed its doors, marking the end of an era.

Other smokestack industries in Duluth's western neighborhoods struggled and soon followed U.S. Steel's lead.

Within a decade, unemployment reached nearly 15 percent. A once-active air base was gone, and iron ore mining north of Duluth was about to come to a virtual standstill. That sent shock waves through the shipping, trucking and railroad industries. Downtown stores were empty and rental space was plentiful.

Duluthians once again banded together, however, forced to weather yet another economic storm.

City leaders looked to Duluth's green hills and blue lake for a fresh start. Tourists were already cruising through town on their way to hot fishing spots up the North Shore. There must be a way, Duluthians thought, to slow down the tourists and their money. Over the next ten years, city leaders used federal highway money to line downtown streets with quaint red bricks and old-fashioned streetlights. They remodeled the old Fitger's brewery, turning it into a plush hotel and a series of gift shops. On the waterfront, warehouses and other eyesores were transformed into shops and cafes. A park was built on top of the completed Interstate 35, and skywalks connected many downtown buildings with a new Duluth Entertain-

> *I told the kids it's just like living in a campground.*

ment Convention Center complex.

Today, Duluth is alive again. Its Christmas-light–filled downtown buzzes with businesspeople. Professional baseball has returned. Hospitals, shopping malls, hotels, a zoo and ski hill make the city a regional hub for all of Northeastern Minnesota.

And people are coming back. Northland moving companies say that since the last half of 1992, more people are moving to Duluth than moving away.

"I told the kids it's just like living in a campground," Joan Homstad said in a *Duluth News-Tribune* interview shortly after she and her Duluth-born husband moved back to Duluth. They had lived for 18 years in the Twin Cities, Chicago, and elsewhere and had grown tired of the hustle and bustle of the big-city rat race.

"We had our fill of the Twin Cities and were looking for a more leisurely form of life," said Mark Homstad. "We became concerned, kind of, that the kids were being raised with the problems in the Twin Cities, the crime rate and things like that."

"I've always been an outdoors person so I loved that here," Joan said. "I'm not leaving till retirement."

Today, Duluth is a city that appears to be on the verge of another boom. Young families like the Homstads are rediscovering their hometown. And many others are discovering Duluth for the first time. Stretching 30 miles with the St. Louis River and Lake Superior on one side and tree-covered hills on the other, Duluth has a bright future.

For Fond du Lac, meanwhile, life is still slow. The city's westernmost neighborhood is a sleepy, almost forgotten part of town. Little traffic zips through since the interstate took cars farther west.

There are no stores here, no gas stations, and few buses. There are only the playful children, the relaxed anglers and the bluffs that hold so much of the city's history.

In a lot of ways, Fond du Lac is Duluth at its purest. The way the pioneers found it. The way the Indians knew it. And hopefully, the way we'll someday leave it.

This page: Life on Lake Superior.

Left: *A view of Duluth-Superior Harbor from the* Victory Chimes.
Below: *Northland Vietnam Veterans Memorial.*
Bottom: *The Cargill elevators.*

Brown Stones and the City They Built

In the 1994 Walt Disney movie *Iron Will*, a castle-like building towers over the start of a sled dog race. It's majestic and grand in its portrayal of Winnipeg City Hall.

It's Duluth's old Central High School, a breathtakingly beautiful building with turrets, a theatrically-steep roof, Olympian clock tower—and a rich past.

Perched proudly atop a small grassy knoll, the building is one of the country's best examples of Richardsonian Romanesque-style architecture. But more importantly, the former school is a lasting tribute to a short-lived industry in Duluth: brownstone quarrying. This industry gave Duluth its warm, old-world feel and most of its historic buildings.

And it's an industry whose history reflects the rise and fall of the local economy.

Brownstone quarrying has roots as early as 1855 when Henry Wheeler used brownstone to build the first steam sawmill. With a Mackinaw boat, he floated the stone from Fond du Lac downstream to what is now 46th Avenue West. A year later, brownstone was used to build a lighthouse on

(Continued on page 47)

A stonecutting dock sprang into action in West Duluth and customers hailed Fond du Lac brownstone as a "wonder stone."

QUARRY, FOND DU-LAC

Left: *The remodeled Fitger's Brewery now houses a series of specialty shops.*
Below: *The old Duluth Central High School shows brownstone construction at its finest.*

Left: Take a walk down by the old train depot near 5th Avenue West and Michigan Street. The turreted brick building was built in 1892 and is now the St. Louis County Heritage and Arts Center.
Below: Yes, the Grandma's of the marathon. It's a popular gathering place all year, but the spaghetti feast the night before the race is always an extra-special treat.

The city they built.

Minnesota Point, the sandbar that stretches like a long finger away from the mainland and separates Lake Superior from Superior Bay. The lighthouse remains on the National Register of Historic Places.

Commercial production of the dawn-red sandstone didn't start until 1870 when entrepreneurs Edmund Ingalls, Michael E. Chambers and Charles A. Krause began digging stone from bluffs above the St. Louis River. Chambers used the stone to build a private mansion. Ingalls sold it to contractors who built Duluth's first "skyscraper," a three-story downtown building. Sensing competition, Chambers followed suit and by 1875, a nucleus of brownstone buildings served as the cornerstone of Duluth's first business district.

Bad times halted brownstone production during the mid-1870s. Duluth's economy was completely intertwined with the interests of Jay Cooke, a Philadelphia investor in Duluth real estate and financier of the Northern Pacific Railroad. When Cooke's banking house failed, initiating the Panic of 1873 and six years of depression, the Duluth population dropped from 5,000 to 1,300. Tax delinquencies filled newspaper pages and the Bank of Duluth collapsed.

The brownstone industry remained dormant about five years, rejuvenated in 1879 by a group of Twin Cities men who traveled 150 miles north to place an order at the quarries. They needed stone for a

Union Depot in St. Paul and a Presbyterian church in Minneapolis.

Within a year, as the economy improved, the industry was back on its feet. And within two years, it was booming as downtown Duluth grew from infancy to a thriving business center. A stonecutting dock sprang into action in West Duluth and customers hailed Fond du Lac brownstone as a "wonder stone." The *Duluth Daily Tribune* claimed, "It is certainly true that no better building material was ever used anywhere."

With prosperity and increased work orders came problems. The large, flat-bottomed boats used to haul the stones down the unpredictable St. Louis River often had trouble getting through. Thousands of floating logs sometimes clogged shipping lanes when they'd get away from loggers and tumble down the river unexpectedly. And sandbar-like islands, formed with sawdust from lumber mills, often got in the way. Sometimes the river was simply impassable—as in the summer of 1888 when bad weather and floods destroyed nearly all the buildings in Fond du Lac and brought navigation to a standstill.

But the industry persevered as brownstone was needed to expand a growing Duluth.

The industry peaked during a building boom in the early 1890s. Quarries employed 150 men and couldn't fill orders fast enough. Lavish apartments, expansive churches, grand theaters, a new

city hall, jail and police station were all built during this boom. Schools, mansions and giant hotels went up. Duluth was suddenly an elaborate, thriving city filled with beautiful stone buildings.

"The crowning achievement of the brownstone era was the completion of Central High School, which was opened for classes on

It is certainly true that no better building material was ever used anywhere.

September 5, 1892," William D. Coventry wrote in his 1987 book about the industry. "A massive Richardsonian style structure, it was similar in design to H.H. Richardson's Allegheny County Courthouse in Pittsburgh."

Today, the building houses Duluth School District offices and is the city's largest remaining brownstone structure.

Casting late afternoon shadows that nearly reach the shores of Lake Superior, old Central is one of the city's most recognized landmarks, and is still a symbol of Duluth.

Above: Grandma's Marathon attracts thousands to the North Shore every year.
Top right: Great places to walk…
Right: …and great places to study.

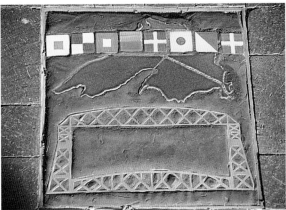

Above: The importance of the lake shows even in a sidewalk tile.
Right: Park Point attracts a crowd on any warm day.
Top: The Morgan Park neighborhood has been a part of Duluth since 1942, but it still has the feel of a separate city. Tucked quietly away from busy Grand Avenue, it is a community truly preserved in time.

A Sense of Neighborhood

Piled high just west of downtown, there's a mountain of black, jagged rock that geologists say has been here more than a billion years. The rock is part of Duluth's massive gabbro formation, the likes of which are found only a couple of other places on earth.

Duluthians call the mountain simply "Point of Rocks." For years they've driven around it, moving fallen chunks aside when necessary. They've scaled its faces and stood on top to enjoy breathtaking views of the St. Louis River as it spills into Lake Superior. A few built homes on the rocks—but only a few. And some discovered copper and silver inside the coarse-grained stone. But no one ever thought there was enough to mine.

Point of Rocks has been more than just a geological treasure or an unusual downtown landmark, however. It was, and in some ways still is, a kind of unofficial dividing point in Duluth. The unspoken but understood border between the East and the West, between the so-called haves and have-nots, between the working class and the wealthy "cake eaters."

East and West is the most obvious division in Duluth.

But there are others. From its earliest roots, Duluth has been a city of neighborhoods. A city shaped by once-separate communities stretched in a straight line along Lake Superior and the St. Louis River. There are ethnic neighborhoods and small burbs filled with people who worked in the nearby smokestack industry. There are those who settled along the shores of the big lake, and those who chose to live over the hill.

For decades, Duluth's divisions have given its residents another identity and a definite source of pride. Duluthians one and all, but there are more than a few residents who won't hesitate to let you know they're from the Raleigh Street neighborhood, or from Denfeld, Central Hillside, Endion, Congdon Park, or any of the other neighborhoods.

Good-natured intracity rivalries have resulted, as have misconceptions about people who live on the other end of town.

These are neighborhoods identified not by the streets or avenues that border them, but by the people who settled them and live in them, or sometimes by the rock formations, streams or hills that make them unique. In some cases, neighborhoods are named for something as simple as the animals that once grazed there. Such is the case with a little-known neighborhood called Goat Hill.

City leaders recognize 29 different neighborhoods. In the beginning, though, there were just 11. The "original 11" were actually townsites.

Fur traders, voyagers and missionaries were the first to find out why an Ojibwe chief once called this part of the world "the center of all good things."

Daniel Greysolon Sieur du Lhut, or Duluth, set up a camp in Fond du Lac, which today is Duluth's westernmost neighborhood. It was the first white settlement at the western tip of Lake Superior, and eventually included fur trading posts and an Ojibwe mission school.

Fond du Lac is a French name interpreted by the British to mean "head of the lake," a tag that sticks to this day.

Other traders and missionaries made their homes in Fond du Lac, including Presbyterian minister and teacher Edmund F. Ely. He eventually moved across St. Louis Bay to a one-room shanty in Superior, Wisconsin. But often he paddled his birch bark canoe back across the bay to the Minnesota territory. There, he'd climb a rocky hillside through heavy timber and gaze longingly at the lake and shoreline. There was a common notion in Superior that one would be "crazy" to build homes on that "pile of rocks" across the bay. But Ely envisioned a great city here. He bought land from two squatters and convinced a St. Paul businessman to build a sawmill. A handful of log homes were fitted together and Oneota, as it was named by another settler, was started.

Appropriately, Oneota is an Indian name that means "the rock from which the people sprang."

The tiny village was a seven-mile canoe ride down the St. Louis River from Fond du Lac, and be-

A tour boat chugs up the St. Louis River past Duluth's westernmost neighborhood, Fond du Lac, during the heyday of the neighborhood.

Above: *Congdon filled Glensheen—his 39-room home—with Oriental rugs, rich oak paneling, textured English leather ceilings, wall coverings of damask made from goat's hair, and 15 fireplaces.*
Facing page: *Autumn from the air.* LARRY MAYER

came the second white settlement in the area. The other nine original settlements started much the same way—by clusters of pioneers who leaned on each other to survive harsh winters and to settle a rugged land:

• Rice's Point, a sawmill town whose inhabitants desperately wanted to be the seat of St. Louis County. They changed the name of their village to the more stately Port Byron and argued that their location between what is now West Duluth and Minnesota Point made them the most centrally located settlement. Their efforts failed, at least until they became part of Duluth.

• Portland, whose streets originally ran on a slant exactly north and south, rather than straight up and down the hillside Duluth is built on. The streets were straightened to match the rest of the area. A park named Portland Square still sits at 10th Avenue East and East Fourth Street, the heart of the original village.

• Fremont, which amazingly enough was built on a floating bog. After the Duluth ship canal was dug through Minnesota Point, a chunk of Fremont was sucked through the canal and floated out into Lake Superior. "In a spirit of patriotism, two men from Duluth took a boat and chased the island until they had intercepted it," Anne Stultz Bailey wrote for a 1976 book about Duluth. "One of them climbed to a high branch of one of the tallest trees of Fremont Island and lashed "Old Glory" firmly to the stout limb. The wanderlustful island then continued on its heedless way, leaving the two men to gaze at the flag of the United States fluttering in the breeze."

Amazingly, when the wind shifted, the island returned, crashed into shore and disintegrated.

• Belville, named for J.B. Bell, who finished building a cabin started by three Superior men who gave up their claim—and stopped building their cabin—when they didn't have enough food for lunch one day. It wasn't the best-planned land grab. And some still joke that it was the area's first labor strike. Belville is the origins of what is today Duluth's easternmost neighborhood, Lakeside.

• Endion, which was about a half-mile east of Portland, was started so that "capitalists doing business in Superior" could have a place to live.

• North Duluth, Cowell's Addition, and Middleton were staked out on or near Minnesota Point, the fingerlike sandbar that separates the Duluth-Superior harbor from Lake Superior. Today, the sandbar is known as Minnesota Point. One road stretches its length and ends at a large park. Joggers, bikers, in-line skaters and sun worshippers flock to the Point each summer.

• Duluth was where much of downtown Duluth still is today.

When early settler Fred Smith got his first look at Duluth on Christmas morning, 1869, he described it as "The haphazard, scraggly and repellant settlement of that time. A mixed combination of Indian trading post, seaport, railroad construction camp and gambling resort altogether wild, rough, uncouth and frontier-like."

It's much prettier now.

As the original eleven merged to become Duluth, the city took off. Waves of immigrants poured into a city that came to be known as "Little Scandinavia." Swedes, Germans and Norwegians are still the largest nationality groups here. Next are Finns and English-speaking Canadians. Depending on the wave of immigration, though, different groups have been prominent at different times. There were the French Canadians, the Scottish, Irish, German, Italian, Polish and the Slavic, which include Serbs, Slovenes and Croats.

Different groups usually settled together, often around their church. Some traces of old residential patterns are still noticeable, but most aren't obvious. Duluth has become a true melting pot.

There was a time, however, when Finns and Jews filled nearly every home below Superior Street near the ship canal. Germans settled in the East Hillside and Central Hillside, later sharing their neighborhoods with Poles. Italians built homes around their church on 10th Avenue West. French immigrants also lived out west, many around what is today Lincoln Park.

One of the first Swedish neighborhoods was on the bayfront near Garfield Avenue.

Most Duluthians chose homesites for more practical reasons, however. Before cars and paved streets and easy transportation, most folks lived where they worked, no matter who their neighbors were.

Morgan Park was built in the early 1900s to house workers at the new multimillion-dollar U.S. Steel plant. Gary-New Duluth, Smithville and Irving sprang up as a cement plant, furniture factory and other small and large industries joined the steel plant in western Duluth.

Riverside was built during the two world wars to house shipbuilders along the St. Louis River.

Most of these "company towns" were complete with their own grocery stores, schools, movie theaters and playgrounds. All within easy walking distance. Some had their own police forces, fire protection and government. And each was filled with hardworking, blue-collar people who took pride in their homes and looked out for their neighbors.

George D. Johnson grew up out here and still lives in a tidy bungalow in West Duluth where he makes jigs for walleye and trout fishing.

Like his father, Johnson worked in the steel plant. He was elected mayor during the 1950s and '60s and later worked as a columnist for the *Duluth News-Tribune*.

"My wife and I were married 11 years before we ever

Each was filled with hard-working, blue-collar people who took pride in their homes and looked out for their neighbors.

bought a car," he said, referring to the years he lived in Morgan Park. "We didn't need one. The grocery store was within walking distance, the post office was within walking distance, the bank was within walking distance. Everything was within walking distance." And streetcars or the railroad could take you downtown.

"I've always liked the lifestyle here," said Johnson, 77, who turned down a high-powered job in Washington D.C. after his last term in the mayor's office. He just

couldn't leave, he said. "It's just that I spend a lot of time in the woods bird hunting, and I've got a little boat with a little motor that I can drag into the water when I want to. I like that."

Duluth has changed a lot during Johnson's lifetime. But the neighborhoods have stayed much the same, he said. They've always been unique, often anchored by schools or churches, but always part of the bigger city. And there's always been that west and east split.

"Duluth used to be considered as divided in half with the hotsy-totsy types, the quote, better element living east of the Point of Rocks and us poor folks living in the west," Johnson said. He grinned, then continued: "They were afraid of us. We always thought they had the notion that we were big tough guys who worked like tigers stripped to the waist, you know.

"But for the last few years of my life I've realized there's as many poor people out east as there are here."

West Duluth dentist Jim Westman has always agreed. The east-west is more in people's minds than in reality. "Among school kids, there was always that perceived split, I suppose. I'm sure they had their names for us and we had our names for them. West was west and east was east, and we only met on the football field," he said.

Above: *Congdon Creek Falls.*
Facing page: *Canal Park with Hillside in the background.* JACK RENDULICH

Morgan Park.

But too much has been made of the differences between east and west, said Westman, 45. He prefers to talk about qualities the entire city shares.

"For me it's as typical an all-American town as you can find. There's still a lot of strength in the feeling of neighborhood pride here," said Westman, who also followed in his father's footsteps to become a dentist. "There's an aw-ful lot of warmth in West Duluth. I've always loved that. It's not the place that makes it so appealing. It's the people that you meet here. It's a group of very warm and friendly and caring people. There are just so many people who are willing to go the extra mile for you."

The western end of Duluth is still blue-collar. There aren't as many belching smokestacks as there used to be. But a paper mill, paper recycling plant and busy industrial parks keep the neighborhoods tied to their past. Young families are breathing life back into old homes. And the old downtown area of West Duluth buzzes once again. "It's a real rebirth. A real phoenix. A real renaissance," Westman said.

As the neighborhoods out west developed, shopkeepers, printers, cabinetmakers and families that depended on two incomes lived downtown near their jobs and near good crosstown transportation. Narrow city lots are still filled with two-story duplexes around downtown. There are also a lot of three-story apartment houses and small businesses with apartments above them.

The wealthy store owners, lawyers and bankers lived in the suburbs out east and over the hill. Attracted by developers who encouraged them "to get away from the roar and hum of the city," streetcar suburbs like Lakeside, Lester Park, Glen Avon and Hunter's Park quickly filled with successful Duluth businessmen and their families. The suburbs remain Duluth neighborhoods today.

Connected by streetcars that were originally pulled by donkeys or horses and electrified in 1890, the tree-lined suburbs were much like suburbs today. During the week, workers commuted into town; and on weekends, they tended to their lawns, built bonfires

It's the people that you meet here. It's a group of very warm and friendly and caring people. There are just so many people who are willing to go the extra mile for you.

and skated on the ice. They got together for ice cream socials or to play cards.

In the summer, there was baseball. And in the winter, there were sleigh rides. In short, neighbors relied on each other for entertainment in those days before television and automobiles and video games.

"There were no strangers. Everyone knew everyone else,"

Lakeside native Georgia Everest wrote about her village in 1953. "The Short Line [commuter train] served as the melting pot of the community. The villagers were like one happy family. It was a group of God-fearing people interested in their homes and in their families.

"Life was not what would be called exciting," she wrote, "but living was wholesome."

The Village of Lakeside is a little different from most of Duluth's streetcar suburbs. It grew up on the edge of the North Shore wilderness long before land developers wooed the wealthy away from downtown. Its English-sounding streets were named by Hugh McCulloch of London, back when there were only a handful of pioneering families living along winding, country roads near the shore of Lake Superior. In 1889, 185 villagers crowded into the tiny schoolhouse and voted unanimously to incorporate their Village of Lakeside.

The settlement was five miles from downtown. And because there were no paved roads, business people, shoppers, and high school students rode the Short Line train into the city. The train ran six times a day.

Movie theaters, drugstores, a town hall and a firehouse were built over the years. Oil lamps illuminated streets that filled with children each evening to watch firefighters exercise the horses that pulled their trucks.

As in most of Duluth's neigh-

59

JACK RENDULICH

JACK RENDULICH

Above: *Urban sprawl has been controlled as much by open space as it has by tough economic times and rock outcroppings that are nearly impossible to build on. But that doesn't mean Duluth's city leaders didn't carefully plan for parks and green space.*
Right: *Indulging in sunrise at the mouth of the Lester River.*

Above: *The northern lights present a dramatic winter show over Lake Superior.* **Left:** *Autumn close-up.*

borhoods, getting fresh water was a problem. But in Lakeside, where Lake Superior stretched out of sight just beyond everyone's front yard, it was especially frustrating. Some villagers had their own wells, but most people bought water from wagons that were filled at the lake in the morning and then peddled door-to-door.

Village leaders struggled with issues typical to most neighborhoods, including street and sidewalk repairs, and how best to provide electricity, sewer lines, and police and fire protection.

Faced with mounting bills, village leaders joined other streetcar neighborhoods and small western towns by reluctantly accepting Duluth's offer to consolidate. They joined their larger neighbor in 1893 with only one request—that Lakeside remain dry. To this day, there are no bars or liquor stores in Duluth's easternmost neighborhood.

A more typical streetcar suburb was Duluth Heights, which was laid out over the hill by the Highland Improvement Company in 1891. The housing developers took what was once described as a small, grassy lake and graded gravel roads across it. They lined those roads with wooden plank sidewalks and street lamps, and then took out ads in the newspaper, offering free lunch and music to anyone who would listen to their sales pitch for the $150 to $300 lots.

They had plenty of takers, including the family of John

People who worked downtown got there by riding the Highland Street Car Line west to the top of Duluth's famous Incline Railway, which carried riders up and down the Duluth hillside.

Fritzen, who moved into Duluth Heights when he was just four years old.

"There was mud and standing water all over," he wrote, remembering the first time he saw his new home. "When we walked on the plank sidewalks, water squirted up through the cracks."

Duluth Heights became a classic residential suburb, though. A heavily Scandinavian community, the center of all activity was the church and the fire hall. The latter was built in the late 1890s because Duluth firefighters were two miles away and on the lower side of the Duluth hillside. Homes were well

built but with little insulation. Only a few had foundations or basements. The only nighttime light came from kerosene lamps and wood burners. Neighbors who had cows sold milk to those who didn't. And a doctor and nurse regularly rode to the new neighborhood on the streetcars to care for the ill.

People who worked downtown got there by riding the Highland Street Car Line west to the top of Duluth's famous Incline Railway, which carried riders up and down the Duluth hillside.

Rides cost five cents.

Those who *did* venture onto city streets often found hazardous conditions. Fritzen wrote, "Snow plowing was almost nonexistent and hand shovelers did the bulk of the work in keeping roads and streets open."

Those early streets included Central Entrance, which today is one of Duluth's busiest roads, carrying motorists into town from the north.

"Our roads were very primitive in the early days," Fritzen wrote. "The first Central Entrance was a narrow dirt road called the County Road. It was dusty in dry weather and muddy when it rained. There was barely room for two cars to meet."

The city's earliest link to the gold and iron ore mines up north wasn't Central Entrance, however. It was the Old Vermilion Trail, which was cut from Duluth to Lake Vermilion by George R.

Stuntz; it passed through what is today the Hunter's Park/Glen Avon neighborhoods. They, too, were streetcar suburbs that developed over the Duluth hillside. Just a few miles beyond Duluth Heights, the neighborhoods were first settled by pioneers Angus McFarlane, his brother-in-law Ronald Hunter and Hunter's brother James. The Hunter brothers were in the banking and investment business and were drawn away from the hustle of the growing city by the woods and the trout-filled streams just outside of town. Streets were surveyed and laid out in 1891, their names reflecting the brothers' Scottish heritage.

Lots were sold and houses were built—including the cozy home that Hugh and Cheryl Reitan live in today.

Like a lot of their neighbors, the Reitans are a young, professional couple who take pride in preserving their home's rich history and original character. Natural wood floors are bathed by sunlight that pours in through large front windows. They've remodeled the kitchen and decorate with wood furniture.

While sipping cups of cappuccino, the Reitans boast about their neighborhood, sounding the way one would imagine the Hunter brothers sounded more than a hundred years ago.

"We like this neighborhood a lot. There are a lot of beautiful woods nearby," said Cheryl, who works in public relations for the nearby College of St. Scholastica. "It's just so picturesque and beautiful with all the woods and the streams.

"The neighborhood just has a feel to it," she said. "Soon after we first moved here we had a block party. We knew half the people, but we got to meet the other half that way. You don't find that everywhere. You certainly don't have that in the bigger cities.

"It's a family neighborhood and people want to keep it that way."

To really get a feel for their white-collar neighborhood, Cheryl and Hugh—who is an architect and president of the Duluth Preservation Alliance—say you have to bike or walk through it. They recommend strolling slowly past the old stone homes built by the Hunter brothers. The stately homes today are kind of unofficial neighborhood boundaries. Then be sure to ride or walk through the University of Minnesota-Duluth campus. Go past a rocky hillside that's easy to spot in the not-too-far distance, and finally head through wooded Hartley Field.

"Duluth's fascinating," Cheryl said. "It still has some of those small-town niceties to it. And the neighborhoods are like small towns themselves."

Not as much as they used to be, but Duluth's neighborhoods certainly have maintained their own feel, their own identity and their own qualities.

From the quiet flow of the St. Louis River in Riverside to the brisk Lake Superior breezes that sweep across Minnesota Point to the bears and deer that sometimes wander into Kenwood to rummage through garbage cans, Duluth is a community of different histories that somehow has grown into one.

Gone are the days when families had to walk to the store. Neighborhood grocery stores still exist, but most Duluthians shop at large-chain supermarkets or in malls downtown or over the hill near Duluth Heights.

Gone are the days when families met at church or school for a party or ice cream social. Some still do, but not because it's the only place they can get to for fun. These days, Broadway shows play the Duluth Entertainment Convention Center and entertainment abounds throughout the city. The city still has an occasional skating party or sleigh ride, but they're more nostalgic now than recreational.

And gone are the days when people commute to work on streetcars. Like the rest of modern America, Duluthians live where they want and drive to work. Or to a baseball game. Or to the theater.

The neighborhoods are still here, however. And so is the neighborhood pride. And they'll probably be here as long as the creeks and hills and ancient rock formations that define them.

Solitude is always easy to find without traveling far from the city.

An Urban Wilderness

Think of Duluth as an oblong diamond wrapped in color. On two sides are the blues of the St. Louis River and Lake Superior. On the other two sides are the greens of forests, wilderness-like areas, golf courses and city parks. From the steep, rocky cliffs that stretch high above western neighborhoods to the winding Lester River out east, the diamond is wrapped in a luxurious ring of open space unofficially known as Duluth's "Greenbelt."

Leaning against a wall in the city planner's office, a large map details the open spaces. There are many of them. Sprawling green blotches that line the edges of town and drip toward the big lake. In all, more than 60 percent of the city is undeveloped, Planner Jerry Kimball said. That's about two times as much park space and open space as other cities of Duluth's size. There's a little more than an acre of park land for every seven Duluth residents.

Call it an urban wilderness.

Duluth appears to be as much on the edge of a frontier today as it did when French explorers first came to trade beaver pelts with the Indians. Most Duluthians live near playgrounds, hockey rinks or baseball fields. Most can bike to a bubbling stream to cool off on a hot summer day. And most can easily take a walk in woods that are filled with deer, bear and the occasional moose.

All without leaving town.

The notion of a Greenbelt comes from London, whose leaders, some 70 years ago, recognized that preserving open space was a good way to control urban sprawl.

In Duluth, urban sprawl has been controlled as much by open space as it has by tough economic times and rock outcroppings that are nearly impossible to build on. But that doesn't mean Duluth's city leaders didn't carefully plan for parks and green space.

"This was going to be the Zenith City of the North, after all," Anne Paine Williams said as she drove her Jeep slowly from park to park on a warm, winter afternoon.

She has more than a passing interest in the city's parks. Her father was Rodney Paine, the parks superintendent under S.F. Snively, the mayor responsible for creating dozens of city parks prior to World War II. And her great grandfather was George B. Sargent, who owned much of the eastern end of the city and whose son William donated what is today Lester Park.

As she drove her old Jeep down a steep, slushy road, she explained that Duluth's desire to preserve green space started long before Snively was voted into office in 1921. It was born prior to the turn of the 20th century when city leaders felt that a world-class park system was needed to attract investors from out East.

Tall pines and oaks lined the creek on both sides, creating a thick forest that somehow didn't seem out of place in the middle of town.

JACK RENDULICH

Right: *A young skier crests the hill at Spirit Mountain.*
Below: *Upper Amity River Rapids, Seven Bridges Road.*

CONRAD BLOOMQUIST

Whatever the season, Minnesota Point offers an impressive place for a walk.

"The city was attractive, but it was wild," Paine Williams said. Potential investors "saw the city as a wilderness with an unforgiving climate." Certainly not the kind of place civilized people would live. And not the kind of place they'd want to invest money.

City leaders figured that a managed park system could help change that notion. They envisioned a long, winding road along the top of Duluth's hillside, and another along the shores of Lake Superior. The two roads would be connected like a picket fence by the dozen or so creeks and rivers that bubble down the Duluth hillside. And each road itself would connect strings of green space and command breathtaking views of the big lake. Nature would be preserved in a civilized and attractive way, the city leaders thought.

They hired professional park planners and the vision began to take shape.

"This is what they were trying to do. You can see the vision here," Paine Williams said as she motored slowly uphill along Tischer Creek in eastern Duluth. Tall pines and oaks lined the creek on both sides, creating a thick forest that somehow didn't seem out of place in the middle of town. "When I was growing up, this was all walking trails and bridle trails. If you were fortunate enough to own a horse."

Paine Williams grew up in what is today Duluth's Lakeside neighborhood. She moved away when she got married, but returned when her husband passed away.

As a girl, she remembers her father telling her how mansions were supposed to someday line the shores of Lake Superior. And how Lakeside was created to house the commoners who would

> *Filled with a few scrubby trees, unmowed grass and lots of nature, it's a forgotten blotch of green on the Greenbelt map in City Hall. Few people probably even realize it's a city park.*

serve the wealthy. He told her about the birth of the parks and instilled in her a love for her hometown.

"The idea was to keep pock-ets of wilderness," she said, pushing her foot against the accelerator. The old Jeep climbed the Duluth hillside before turning onto Skyline Parkway, the top-of-the-hill road that became a reality.

"One hundred years later, the view really hasn't changed," she said, her eyes wandering downhill and out over Lake Superior. "You're looking over a few more houses, but you can still see that glorious lake.

"I came back to be on that lake. There's something spiritual about it. There's always been a pull for me. I've been to the Pacific Ocean and the Atlantic Ocean and I was impressed. But they just didn't have the pull. I don't know what it is."

The Jeep rolled back down the hill, past several neighborhood parks. Each a square block in size, some featured playgrounds, hockey rinks or basketball hoops. Others were just a few trees and brush. All were built for the people who lived around them.

Paine Williams' father was responsible for creating many of Duluth's parks, as was Mayor Snively, under whose leadership the 19.5-mile Skyline Parkway was built. W.K. Rogers was the first president of the Duluth Park Board. He wrote the city's first park plan. His vision was carried out in later years by Judge C.R. Magney, Luther Mendenhall and others.

And then there were the many Duluthians who helped Mayor Snively in his quest "to create one of the most beautiful cities in America."

They donated acre after acre of land, all to be preserved as parks. They were people with now-common Duluth names like Enger, Ordean, Prindle, and Merritt.

They were also everyday people like William W. Strickland, who in 1925 donated a tiny one-third acre tract of land just below Mesaba Avenue. In the deed he stipulated that "the above granted premises shall be forever maintained as a park," that the city shall never permit "the parking of cars, the storage of materials, the erection of buildings, the vending of refreshments," but may allow "the erection of a band stand, seats, resting places, pagodas or weather shelters."

Today, Strickland Park is like a lot of Duluth's 105 parks. Filled with a few scrubby trees, unmowed grass and lots of nature, it's a forgotten blotch of green on the Greenbelt map in City Hall. Few people probably even realize it's a city park.

"Open space is close to just about everybody in the city. That makes it a good city for the human spirit," said Kimball, the city planner. "You don't have the urban sprawl all over the place. Duluth really hasn't suffered from the suburbia syndrome. And a lot of that is because of the Greenbelt."

In addition to parks, the Greenbelt also includes golf courses, ski trails, hiking trails, homes on large lots, cemeteries, forest preserves and any other undeveloped land.

Like a sponge, the open areas help prevent flooding in the spring and fall. In the summer, they are places to picnic or meditate. And on bright winter afternoons, they are places for people like Anne Paine Williams to take a drive.

She was heading home soon. But first, she wanted to nose the Jeep past Lester Park in the eastern end of town. Outside the Jeep's windows, rock-lined banks could be seen towering over the Lester River. Jagged hills and thick forests zipped by on either side of the road.

"This is rugged stuff here," Paine Williams said. "It's not a typical urban park. It's not what a lot of people around the country think of in terms of what a park should be. But here, it's just another pocket of wilderness."

JACK RENDULICH

Lake Superior at the mouth of the Cascade River.

Lake Breezes

A fluffy, almost postcard-like snow swirled across Duluth streets that Halloween afternoon in 1991.

We knew it was coming. But the storm that eventually dumped a record 37 inches of snow seemed so innocent when it first started.

Snow accumulated slowly that afternoon. On the shoulders first. Then between car tires, making the roads look like those sheets of lined paper children use when learning to write. But it was just another fall dusting. Nothing unusual.

By evening, however, the roads were as white as typing paper, and only four-wheel drive vehicles were moving. Pumpkins, and the front steps they decorated, were buried in bright snow. Few children ventured out to ask neighbors for candy. Even fewer adults realized the storm had only just begun.

On Friday morning, a foot of snow was being whipped around by bitterly cold 40 m.p.h. winds. It was difficult, if not impossible, for anyone to get to work. And when another nine inches of snow fell during that unbelievably gray day, it made it even more difficult to get home.

Some workers were stranded downtown for two or three days. Belly-deep drifts kept them from pushing their way up the Duluth hillside to their homes. Those who did make it, dug tunnels to corner markets and used plastic sleds to pull home milk and bread. Playful children made the best of the storm. They swooshed down Duluth's steep avenues without having to worry about cars.

The low rumble of thunder and bright flashes of lightning filled the skies before the storm finally let up Saturday evening.

Snowplow drivers were left with the thankless job of cutting paths through narrow roadways as motorists emerged from their cozy homes to shovel cars out of snowy tombs.

> *Storms are hard to predict, adding to the area's reputation as a rugged place with an unforgiving climate.*

Even before the roads were cleared of an estimated 190 million cubic feet of snow, the media dubbed the occurrence "Megastorm," a label that stuck.

"We knew it was coming," meteorologist Jim Christenson told a *Duluth News-Tribune* reporter a year later. "There were winter storm warnings out. But no one could predict quite the amounts that we received."

A lot of Duluth storms are hard to predict, adding to the area's reputation as a rugged place with an unforgiving climate. There's a running joke up here that our weather would kill most people. "Yep," we'll say, our voices brimming with pride as we yank up our snow pants and sniffle toward a frosty sky, "most folks couldn't live through this."

Lake Superior is the leading cause of the unpredictable weather. A constant source of moisture, the largest lake in the world (in surface area) acts a little like a heater in the winter and a lot like an air conditioner in the summer. Just ask any irritated Duluth visitor forced to wear a winter jacket to watch Fourth of July fireworks. Or those who forget to bring jackets at all. They complain to Duluthians who nod politely and grin knowingly.

"I remember whole summers when we couldn't sit outside on the grass because it was too cold," said Rosalyn Dryke, 79. She grew up in Duluth's East Hillside neighborhood and now lives with her husband in a spacious apartment near Miller Hill Mall. "The air was real cold when it came off that lake. But I still went swimming."

That's the way Duluthians are. They'll wear shorts and break out bicycles the first day water drips off snow-covered rooftops. They'll fish all year, even if it means standing carefully on a snow-cov-

The March 1985 blizzard dumped tons of snow on Minnesota Point and left residents stranded for several days. A boy walks between huge snowdrifts toward the Aerial Bridge as others shovel through drifts to their cars.

Duluth weather is seldom a good reason to cancel outdoor plans, but often a reason to make them.

Left: *A typical Duluth winter smile.*
Below: *A musher is interviewed before the start of the John Beargrease Sled Dog Marathon, which runs each winter along Lake Superior's North Shore between Duluth and Grand Portage. The race starts in the Ordean Junior High School Stadium. The Beargrease is the largest such race in the lower 48 states.*
Bottom: *A winter day, a rink—enough said.*

GREG RYAN & SALLY BEYER

ered shoreline or drilling holes through the ice. And they'll play softball late into the fall; never mind the early darkness and snow showers. It seems the weather rarely ruins outdoor plans.

Not in the winter and not in the summer, a season when the phrase "cooler by the lake" rings true. There are summer days when a cool lake breeze will keep it at 40 degrees on the beach, while a bright sun will push temperatures over the Duluth hillside to near 80 degrees.

"I've always been surprised that Lake Superior's climate hasn't been studied more," said Bruce Watson, an independent meteorologist from Roseville, Minnesota. "It's unique because the [lake's] water temperature is near 39 degrees all year round. You don't get your normal land and sea relationships. The weather can change very quickly there. The wind only has to change a little bit off that lake."

The lake can push rolling walls of fog up the Duluth hillside or conjure up unexpected squalls of snow.

The flatlands to the west are as much to blame for snowstorms and thunderstorms that slam into Duluth. Each winter, Alberta Clippers dump heavy snowfalls on Duluth and drive down wind chills.

"They can come out of Canada like a freight train," said George Kessler, a meteorologist for KBJR-TV6 in Duluth.

Despite the storms, the weather in some ways is Duluth's most endearing quality. Sure, winters last too long, and it's tough to endure a late spring snowfall knowing that in Milwaukee and Chicago they're already playing golf and softball. And yes, it's tough to live through days and even weeks of plug-in-the-car, sub-zero temperatures. But there's nothing more reassuring and heartwarming than the warmth of the sun on your face after more than six months of snow and ice and cold. Or that first day of fishing in the spring—a day many Duluthians dream about as though it were something just out of their grasp. It somehow makes it all worthwhile.

Duluth is a city where nice weather isn't wasted. It's probably not as rare as it seems, but sunshine is relished. And no matter who you are, no matter where you are, if it's nice outside, you just have to take advantage.

It's no secret. Visitors flock to the city in the summer to escape the heat down south. And they come in the winter to swoosh along mile after mile of cross country ski trail.

"The best cross-country skiing we've done in a long time was near Duluth after it snowed 26 inches in 24 hours," Tom Walsh wrote the *News-Tribune* from his home in West Branch, Iowa, in January 1994. "Having experienced Duluth's recent record

snowfall—and having enjoyed it thoroughly—we've decided to offer our services, free of charge, as the Duluth Chamber of Commerce Poster Family. I mean, how many families choose to move to Duluth because of the weather, eh?"

Still, when most of the country hears about Duluth, it's on the Weather Channel and usually because of another monster snowstorm or because we're the coldest spot in the nation that day. "Even colder than Alaska," the forecaster will say, smirking.

Folks are rugged in Duluth, all right. They're proud, survivalist types who'd like nothing better than to bring that grinning forecaster to town. See how long he'd last.

Everyone has a favorite weather story here, too. A favorite tale of which storm was the worst, which one was the most surprising, or which one was the most humorous.

The Megastorm produced a lot of stories. There was the woman and her husband who somehow got snowbound for several days with her ex-husband and his new girlfriend. There was the Superior couple who had a baby in the middle of the storm. A snowplow had to clear the way for an ambulance to get to their home. And then there were the snowplow drivers themselves, the men and women we all depend on to free us from our driveways. They got stuck too.

Other storms have also been

the subjects of countless retellings, as well.

The Armistice Day Snowstorm of 1940 is perhaps the most famous.

The summer was mostly sunny and dry that year. And as duck hunters took to the woods and marshes in the fall, the weather held. Some forecasters warned a storm was on the way that fateful November weekend. But with temperatures pushing the mid-40s, few people took them seriously. It was so balmy in Claremont, Minnesota, in fact, that Wrenshall, Minnesota, Mayor Hugh Line—then 19—took off his shirt while picking gladiola bulbs on the farm where he was working.

That was Friday.

"On Saturday, it started misting a little bit," Line said in a *Duluth Herald* interview years later. "The same on Sunday. It was still fairly warm. And the same Monday morning. Then somewhere close to 11 o'clock it turned to snow. I'll tell you what, inside of half an hour you couldn't see more than 30, 40 feet. It just came—boom!—just like that. And we were running out chasing cattle into the barn."

That same morning near Buffalo, Minnesota, Duluth's Don Henkel saw something so unbelievable that he forgot all about an oncoming storm. "First, you could see this line in the sky, the clouds coming in," Henkel said in a newspaper interview. "And it

The flatlands to the west are as much to blame for snowstorms and thunderstorms that slam into Duluth. Each winter, Alberta Clippers dump heavy snowfalls on Duluth and drive down wind chills.

went from being perfectly calm—a bluebird type of day—to a high wind. Then sleet. Then snow. And then it seemed like every duck in North America came through on that front. We saw not only thousands, millions of waterfowl, but they were close to the ground, just clearing the tops of the trees. And they were so close to each other you could hear wings flap against one another."

Henkel, his father and his uncle could only gaze in wonder through a driving snow at the millions of ducks that blocked out the sky. Eventually, the men hiked to a

farmhouse where they spent the next two days riding out the storm.

In Duluth that morning, rain froze hard to the streets before the heavy snow began. Schools were closed and workers were stranded downtown. Snowdrifts were pushed to the rooftops by 50 m.p.h. winds. Tunnels were dug through the snow to doorways and the Northern Pacific ticket office set up a lost and found for hats blown off by the storm. The wind also played havoc with attempts to spread sand on ice-covered streets. And it ripped away flags that had been placed atop several downtown buildings to mark the start of the annual Red Cross membership drive. Trees toppled under the weight of inch-thick ice. One tree crashed across Superior Street between 15th and 16th Avenues East.

"The Great Armistice Day Snowstorm," as it came to be known, has been described by some historians as the worst storm ever. It was "a white typhoon that burst furiously across the Great Plains and swept all the way to the Atlantic, drifting snow to housetops, sinking ships on the Great Lakes, marooning hunters, and killing 144 people," the *News-Tribune* reported. Almost half the deaths were in Minnesota.

Other snowstorms have rivaled the Armistice Day storm. Longtime Duluth photojournalist Chuck Curtis has seen—and photographed—his share. He took one of his favorite winter weather shots

The sun lights a new day on Superior.

JACK RENDULICH

The Mansion, bed and breakfast in style, just a stone's throw from Glensheen.

in March of 1985. It still hangs in his home. In the now-famous picture, cars are seen rolling slowly and carefully between mountains of snow. On top of one of the mountains, a young man is plunging a shovel into the snow.

He was actually digging *down* to his family's buried car, Curtis said.

"It wasn't a huge blizzard. It's just that the wind blew all the snow off Lake Superior and it all ended up on Park Point," Curtis said. "The snow filled in the streets and it filled in the sidewalks. A lot of people had to get out of their homes through sec-

ond-story windows. And [after the city cleared the streets] the people trying to get to their cars had to dig down to them from the tops of the snowbanks."

Stories told by Curtis and other Duluthians don't always center on snowstorms. In fact, there have been several times when the city was nearly washed into Lake Superior. One of the first was July of 1909.

Thunder crackled across the Duluth skyline that warm midsummer night.

Before long, rain water was pouring down Duluth avenues, washing away roads, grass and trees as it rushed to the bottom of the hill. Timbers, paving blocks, mud and other debris tumbled toward Lake Superior as startled pedestrians scrambled for cover. Two young children drowned when they were swept from their mother's arms. Other tragedies were prevented by quick-thinking men who rolled up their trousers and by women who kicked off their shoes and splashed through the water to save strangers in trouble.

Audiences inside the Bijou Theater near downtown's Lake Avenue didn't know about the storm until muddy floodwaters poured through the aisles. Damage was heavy in the theater and elsewhere downtown. One store was filled above its countertops with water—before the torrent broke through plate glass windows and rushed outside.

Another torrential two-hour rainfall, this one during the summer of 1972, also sent furniture, telephone poles, bricks, lumber and mud cascading down the Duluth hillside toward Lake Superior. The city was declared a major disaster area after nearly three inches of rain fell just after 4 A.M. that Sunday.

As the morning sun rose above Lake Superior, benches and pews floated in chest-deep water in area churches. Large holes were ripped into people's yards. And houses were knocked off their foundations. No one was hurt or killed in the storm, but homes,

businesses, and entire city streets were washed away. A garage knocked off its foundation toppled onto a pickup truck.

Duluth's warmest day was July 14, 1936, when it reached 106.2 degrees. Amazingly—but in true Duluth form—newspaper headlines the next day announced, "Duluth Is An Oasis While Nation

> *It went from being perfectly calm—a bluebird type of day—to a high wind. Then sleet. Then snow. And then it seemed like every duck in North America came through on that front.*

Suffers." During the night, the wind shifted off Lake Superior as it so often does. A cool, almost chilly, breeze blew into town, carrying clouds and rain. Temperatures dropped 41 degrees to a high the next day of just 65 degrees.

The coldest day was recorded on January 2, 1885, when the mercury plummeted to 41 degrees below zero. Without wind chill.

Mark Twain supposedly once said, "The coldest winter I ever spent was a summer in Duluth." It's a common notion. But it's not completely accurate. It's true that Duluth was chosen by President Ulysses S. Grant to be one of the nation's original 24 weather observation stations. It's true that Duluthians are among a chosen few who truly know there is a *big* difference between -5° and -30°. It's also true that Duluthians will play hockey or go ice fishing long after the car's digital clock freezes, and the frozen front seat in the truck feels like plywood.

But it should also be remembered that Duluth's weather isn't as unlivable as Duluthians might have you believe. When something like the "Megastorm" hits, it's not altogether an unwelcome burden. In some ways it's an opportunity for Duluth to show its true character.

Strangers work together to push snow-stalled cars. People with four-wheel-drive vehicles or snowmobiles volunteer to take home snowbound neighbors. And without being asked, people who own snowblowers help out those who don't.

That's just the way Duluth is. And the way of the weather.

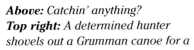

Above: *Catchin' anything?*
Top right: *A determined hunter shovels out a Grumman canoe for a winter goose hunt.*
Right: *Through the woods.*

Watchin' the Wrecks

U.S.150810

The steamer Mataafa *swung broadside across the end of the north pier of the Duluth Canal during the height of the great storm of November 28, 1905. Nine men lost their lives on the vessel.*

COURTESY OF THE DOSSIN GREAT LAKES MUSEUM, DETROIT, MI

Gale force winds howled at the Duluth Coast Guard station when the distressed ship was first spotted.

"One of the people here...saw out the window what looked like a ship barreling into Park Point," a Coast Guard spokesman told the *Duluth News-Tribune* that November evening in 1985.

What the guardsmen saw was the 584-foot *Socrates* running

> *The shipwrecks are a part of the Duluth-Superior harbor that has fascinated generations.*

aground. The ship dragged anchors that proved no match for a Lake Superior nor'easter. It settled into soft sand only 150 feet from shore. Ten-foot waves crashed over its bow that night, making it impossible for tugs to free it. High-powered lamps flooded the deck with light as the crew of 24 sailors could do little but wait for help in the morning light.

For much of the next week, all five of the Great Lakes Towing

Company's tugs shoved and yanked at the *Socrates*, which was on its way to Duluth to pick up a load of wheat bound for Italy. Dredges dug ditches around the ship, but the freighter didn't budge. It rocked in the surf and remained parallel to shore.

Duluthians ate it up. They flocked to Minnesota Point as though it were the first warm day of summer. "It's family folks. People are bringing their kids," one Park Point resident told a *News-Tribune* reporter. "In the summer there's equally as many people."

After a day or two, visitors from other cities arrived, bolstering what is normally a slow month for tourism in Duluth. Traffic backed up on the Point's only road. And officials at the Duluth Convention and Visitor's Bureau—always eager to cash in on a good thing—set up a "shipwreck hot line" and started a shuttle bus to haul the binocular- and camera-wearing curious to the *Socrates*.

Six days later, with a circus-like atmosphere on shore, tugs continued to strain against 650-foot-long lines that were tied to the ship. Other tugs nudged the *Socrates'* bow back and forth, gradually working the stern free of the sandy lake bottom. The ship finally crept about 120 feet forward before picking up speed and running on its own back into Lake Superior. "She's really moving," someone said in the Coast Guard station. Other guardsmen ran to the win-

83

Above: *The light at Canal Park cuts through subzero morning air.*
Left: *An early freeze traps a ship in Lake Superior.*

dow. "That's it. There you go," someone else yelled.

After repairs, the *Socrates* left Duluth on December 6, almost a month after arriving. Though the ship didn't actually sink, many Duluthians considered it a true shipwreck. They jokingly wrote songs, adapting music from the classic Gordon Lightfoot tune, "Wreck of the *Edmund Fitzgerald*." And some even got nostalgic during the summer of 1993 when the *Socrates* returned to the Duluth-Superior harbor—this time with a new name painted across its bow.

The *Socrates* is the latest member of a bittersweet fraternity. Though the Duluth-Superior harbor isn't known for shipwrecks, at least 12 ships have gone down here. The *Socrates* is the only one that sailed away.

One of the first crashed during a November storm in 1905 that included hurricane-force winds. Out on Lake Superior, 26 vessels were damaged or destroyed that fall. Seventeen others were stranded and one sank. At least 33 lives were lost.

In Duluth, thousands of people winced at bone-chilling winds near the ship canal and atop downtown rooftops to marvel at the awesome storm. That's when the iron-laden steamer *Mataafa* appeared in the distance, struggling through a snow squall. The giant laker drove hard for the ship canal and the protection that the Duluth-Superior harbor offered.

But as it approached, wind and currents threw the ship into the north pier. It bounced back into Lake Superior before slamming broadside into the pierhead.

The bundled crowds cried in horror as the *Mataafa* went down

> *The following morning, rescuers reached the broken ship and found 15 crew members who had built a bonfire of hacked-up furniture to stay alive.*

just 150 yards from shore. Its cargo bled a rusty red into the mud-brown, white-capped harbor. And its crew signaled for help from cabins that somehow bobbed in the waves. The storm made it impossible for lifeboats or the U.S. Life Savers to reach the ship. All Duluthians could do was stand vigil on the beach as angry waves rolled over the *Mataafa*, driving it deeper into the water.

The following morning, a day before Thanksgiving, rescuers reached the broken ship and found 15 crew members who had built a bonfire with hacked-up furniture to stay alive. Nine other men either drowned or froze to death in a wreck that nearly all Duluth witnessed.

Large crowds also gathered in 1891 when a passenger boat named *Winslow* caught fire near the Duluth waterfront. The vessel was eventually towed up the St. Louis River where it sank. A few of its timbers remain above water today.

Other Twin Ports shipwrecks weren't as dramatic, Canal Park Marine Museum Director Pat Labadie told the *Duluth News-Tribune* in 1986.

The *M.C. Neff* was a barge that burned accidentally in the St. Louis River near the Oliver Bridge in 1909. It came to rest in just a few feet of water and has been picked over for years by amateur divers and adventuresome children.

The graceful three-masted warship *Essex*, which spent many years in Duluth as a naval militia ship, was towed into Lake Superior in 1930 and burned intentionally. The old ship apparently had passed its time of usefulness. The bottom of the vessel, with its rows of shiny copper spikes, still lies partly on the sand beach near the Superior entry.

A schooner named *Guido Pfister* was abandoned after it hit

the south pier of the Duluth ship canal in 1885. Part of the vessel was salvaged when a new canal was built in 1901, but the rest of it is still there, about halfway down the pier that holds thousands of tourists each year.

The *Thomas E. Wilson*, a whaleback steamer built in Superior, was rammed and sank on the big lake about half a mile from the Duluth ship canal in 1902. Its wreck has been popular among divers who need boats to reach it and have to wait for a northeast wind to push in clear water. The wreck was placed on the National Register as an archaeological site in 1992.

A boat believed to be a ferry named *Oden* is buried under dredge spoils near Duluth's ship canal. It's not known when the ship was abandoned on Minnesota Point.

Several tugboats and barges burned and then sank in 1918 when roaring forest fires reached Lake Superior. Spikes and timbers from some of the vessels are still visible poking through the blue water.

A local ferry, the *Stillman Witt*, carried people across Superior Bay from Duluth's Minnesota Point to Wisconsin's Superior before it was abandoned on the Point. The vessel is still there, buried under sand from years of dredging the harbor bottom.

A passenger and freight steamer called *City of Winnipeg* caught fire in 1881 and was towed behind Minnesota Point. It was abandoned in an area later filled with sand dredged from the harbor bottom. Today, the ship actually lies under the sand peninsula, though no one is quite sure where.

A schooner named *Algonquin* was abandoned in Superior in 1855. It sank into obscurity as well as into the harbor bottom. But there was a time when the *Algonquin* was the only commercial vessel on Lake Superior. Built in 1839, it was the first to portage into the lake past the rapids in Sault Ste. Marie, Michigan.

The wrecks contain little of actual value. None contains sunken treasure or unsalvaged cargo. And most have deteriorated in the harbor's relatively warm water. But the shipwrecks are a part of the Duluth-Superior harbor that has fascinated generations.

"Most people don't have any idea those little bits of archeology are around here," Labadie said in 1986. "Some of them aren't very historical. But others were the *Socrates* of yesteryear. They were really big stories in their day, and they played a big role in the development of our area."

Right: Wherever you look in Duluth, there's a view.
Below: Another Superior denizen.
Bottom: Day begins for all.

PHILIP G. OLSON

Left: Greg Swingley winning the 1991 John Beargrease
Sled Dog Marathon.
Below: Superior ice sculptures.

CONRAD BLOOMQUIST

89

Border Rivalry

The race was on.

The year was 1869. Duluth and Superior, Wisconsin, were both struggling but growing communities, each dreaming of becoming a glamorous and affluent Great Lakes port.

The potential certainly was there. Out East, much of what would become the St. Lawrence Seaway was open and ships carrying goods for the frontier West were already arriving. City leaders in the neighboring towns knew that whoever controlled the shipping traffic, controlled the future.

Superior had an advantage with its natural entry into a harbor protected by a long peninsula. As Duluth leaders talked about digging a channel through their own end of the peninsula, the Army Corps of Engineers gave the apparent nod to the Superior side of the harbor when it decided to build piers at Superior's entry and then dredge a seven-mile channel to Duluth.

Unfortunately for Superior, the big lake had other ideas. A storm trashed the breakwater at Superior's entry even before the work there was completed.

Duluth reacted quickly. Talk of digging a channel turned to action and the formation of the Minnesota Canal and Harbor Improvement Committee. The group was told to "construct and maintain such necessary piers, wharves and landings...as may be deemed necessary for commercial purposes."

In the fall of 1870, a steam dredge began to chew its way through the sandy Duluth peninsula.

Superiorites fumed.

Still stinging after the Lake Superior and Mississippi Railroad built its northern rail line to Duluth rather than Superior, they weren't about to lose shipping as well. They filed suit in federal court to stop the dredging. Legal battles raged into the spring of 1871 as the steam dredge continued its sand munching.

On June 9, U.S. Supreme Court Justice Samuel F. Miller fi-

> *A storm trashed the breakwater at Superior's entry even before the work there was completed.*

nally ordered the Minnesotans to "absolutely desist and abstain from digging, excavating, and constructing...the said canal."

The ruling was telegraphed to Duluth, but it took a federal marshal three days to arrive and execute the order.

Legend has it that in those three days, Duluthians armed with picks and shovels worked around the clock to help the steam dredge move the earth. By the morning of June 12, a small channel was opened. And when the federal marshal finally arrived that afternoon, all he could do was watch helplessly as Duluthians cheered the steam tug *Fero*, the first vessel to pass through the Duluth ship canal.

It was a turning point for the two cities. Duluth grew rapidly after that day, the apparent victor in the race to control both the railroad and shipping. Superior, on the other hand, seemed destined to fall forever into Duluth's shadow.

There was a time when Superior boasted the world's tallest grain elevator. But geography textbooks placed it in Duluth. Superior was also first to offer tours aboard a historical ship when it acquired a retired whaleback freighter. But Duluth stole away visitors when it docked the retired U.S. Steel flagship *William A. Irvin* and offered its own tours. Superior even had plans to develop its waterfront long before Duluth city officials turned a run-down lakeside warehouse district into restaurants, shops and other tourist attractions.

Today, the Twin Ports of Duluth, Minnesota and Superior, Wisconsin coexist somewhat harmoniously. In most ways the two cities are one community. They're connected by two easy-to-cross bridges that span Superior Bay, and by several organizations that call both cities home. The Duluth Symphony Orchestra became the Duluth-Superior Symphony Orchestra in 1974. And when minor league baseball returned to the Twin Ports in 1993, management decided to call their team the Duluth-Superior Dukes.

Still, a good-natured rivalry remains, some of it passed down by generations familiar with the battle for shipping. Some longtime Superior residents even recall being taught in school that Duluth cheated Superior.

High School and college sports teams keep the rivalry fresh each year, if only on the court or field.

For some, that's enough.

For others, it never could be. There are residents in both cities who still take pride in the number of years they can allow to pass before crossing the bridge, who make sure they do all their shopping in their hometown, regardless of price or selection, and who resort to tongue-in-cheek name calling.

Some Duluthians refer to Superiorites as Flatlanders because their city is relatively flat. Or because they live in Wisconsin, they are called Cheeseheads.

A good-natured rivalry remains, some of it passed down by generations familiar with the battle for shipping.

Duluthians, on the other hand are referred to as Cliff Dwellers. Or it's said that the view from the top of Duluth's hillside is so breathtaking because you're looking at Superior and northwestern Wisconsin.

"Why they build some of those houses hanging off the hill is beyond me," Joanne Gidley still jokes about Duluthians. A lifelong Superiorite, her job is to attract conventions and visitors to her hometown.

She said that more and more each year the two cities work together to attract tourists, conventions and businesses to the Twin Ports—not just to Duluth and not just to Superior. Superior leaders have long since gotten over ill feelings for their Minnesota neighbors and have realized that having Duluth next door is good for their own tourism business.

Superior's tourist-attracting slogan is evidence. It proclaims, "Next to Duluth, We're Superior."

"That's a friendly slogan," Gidley said. "Duluth-Superior is a joint destination. When people say they're coming north—and that's the way they always say it, too: 'We're going up north'— they're coming to the area. The bridge is no barrier."

"No matter in which city a dollar is spent, the bottom line is that the dollar stays in the area," said Dave Minor of the Superior-Douglas County Chamber of Commerce. "You still have the rivalry, but most of it is good-hearted."

Like Duluth, Superior is a city with a once proud and strong industrial base. But also like Duluth—and many other cities across the country—the heavy industry disappeared. The city's big railroad yards aren't as noisy as they once were. Downtown is void of any large office buildings. And most of the old wooden ore docks that tower over the harbor are forgotten and slowly being covered over with weeds and trees.

"A lot of people are still waiting for the railroad and ore docks and the other industries to come back. But they're not going to come back," Gidley said. "At one time it definitely was a working class town. But now it has to be geared more toward tourism, whether the local people realize that or not."

Right: Oh, that lake!
Below: Our friend, neighbor, and rival—Superior, Wisconsin.

Facing page: Superior's popular Fairlawn Mansion is open year-round.

Superior hasn't become a vacation hot spot like Duluth partly because of Superiorites' reluctance to let go of the industrial past. Mostly, though, it's been due to a lack of state grants, federal aid and local taxes.

But it is happening. One-fourth of the city's workers held tourism-related jobs in 1993; the same year new home construction jumped 44 percent, Minor said.

Tourism is just starting to take hold.

There are ambitious plans to turn more than ten miles of Superior's waterfront into a vacation playground. The plans include a wooden boardwalk that will run the entire length of the shoreline—from Connor's Point where outdoor festivals are now being held; to Barker's Island with its sprawling marina and handsome hotel; past wetlands, the Nemadji River and Hog Island to the old wooden ore docks that still tower high above the water, a bittersweet reminder of the city's shipping heyday; through the woods to the sandy beaches on Wisconsin Point; and finally to the twin lighthouses that mark the Superior ship canal entry.

Other Superior attractions include 29 city parks, a municipal forest, state parks, snowmobile trails, stock car racing and the 36-hole Nemadji Golf Course.

There's also the S.S. *Meteor*, the last remaining "whaleback" freighter. Launched in 1896, it's now a floating museum docked at Barker's Island. The *Meteor* was a forerunner to the huge Great Lakes freighters that still sail in and out of the Duluth-Superior harbor. Guided tours of the boat are offered daily from May to September.

There's the Fairlawn Mansion Museum, which casts its shadow across Highway 2. Built by Superior's second mayor, timber baron Martin Pattison, the 42-room mansion is a trip in history to the early days of the Great Lakes Victorian elegance.

And there's the Fire House and Police Museum in Superior's East End Old Town. The brick, castle-like building is the last of the city's turn-of-the-century fire stations. It houses antique fire and police equipment and vehicles, including a restored 1906 steam pumper.

"With so much to offer, I certainly see this city moving forward," Gidley said.

As it does, more and more people are certain to discover this often-forgotten corner of northwestern Wisconsin, a city that appears ready to finally emerge from Duluth's shadow. So don't be surprised if more and more bumper stickers pop up in the Midwest proclaiming "I'm A Superior Lover."

The North Shore

It was the kind of night Joyce Klees loves.

The air was crisp, clean and cold. A full moon had turned treetops into silhouettes and Lake Superior was frozen over for the first time in years.

The lake seemed to be calling as Klees grabbed her ice skates and trudged through the glistening snow to the edge of the frozen water.

The greens and blues of northern lights pulsated magically across the sky as her blades cut into the giant lake for the first time.

"People come out on the ice and they just sigh, 'My problems are going to be okay'," Klees said. "People's lives get so busy. The North Shore gives them peace and reminds them of what's simple. There's a sense of connectedness to the universe. It brings peace to me, too."

It was the kind of night Klees yearned for when she first moved to the North Shore in 1978. It was the kind of magical moment that leaves her wondering whether she'll ever leave.

"This feels more like home than anyplace I've ever been," said Klees, who lives near Tofte, an old logging and commercial fishing village. "The forests and the lake have a lot of power that keep me here. There's a great sense of community up here. It's more rugged and more wild than a lot of places. I like that."

Her sense of connection and belonging is common on Minnesota's North Shore, a historically rugged wilderness. People who live here still have a kinship with nature that most of us only dream about. They speak nonchalantly about sharing their yards with moose and deer, and they pay close attention to the way robins and chickadees react to unexpected weather.

It's the kind of woodsy life that visitors to the North Shore can only glimpse. No matter how hard they try.

Each summer, thousands of tourists jam Minnesota Highway 61 as it winds 147 miles from Duluth to the Canadian border at Pigeon River. They come to enjoy the Lake Superior shoreline with its beaches of small flat pebbles, its towering rock cliffs, historic lighthouses, and expansive forests. They drive through quaint, friendly towns with romantic names like Castle Danger, Two Harbors and Grand Portage. Or they stop at state parks to marvel at the beauty of a stream tumbling over tall rock walls and into Lake Superior below.

It's easily one of the most scenic drives in America, causing some visitors to dream about what life would be like living on the shore. But very few ever chase their dream.

Marion Calph did.

The St. Paul, Minnesota, native came to the North Shore in 1983, building a domed house about seven miles south of Schroeder and only a whisper away from Lake Superior. She planned to split her time between the Shore and her home in the Twin Cities.

"But with my income I couldn't afford that," she said. "So I decided to live up here. Most of my friends said, 'you're nuts to live up there where it's so cold.' But I haven't regretted it for a day."

The retired Schroeder Town Clerk loves to spend warm summer afternoons paddling a small square-ended boat out onto the big lake. She often positions herself over a sunken barge, its hull still in perfect view through nine feet of crystal clear water.

"This lake is a world of its own. It mesmerizes me. When I go away, I can't wait to get back to it," said Calph, who also plays handbells for a church in Silver Bay, shops at area garage sales and loves to garden.

It's not what one might call an exciting life. But she said she wouldn't trade it.

"I was born and raised in the city so I never had any connection to nature. Until now," Calph said, gazing reflectively from her home's deck toward the big lake. It looked like a mirror on this perfect spring day.

"I have no other home but here. And I'm going to stay here until I have to leave. I hope that never happens."

A few miles up the shore, Steve Krueger ignored the lake as he sauntered slowly across his

GREG RYAN & SALLY BEYER

Above: *A whitetail doe at home.*
Left: *The Lester River is a favorite for fly fishing.*
Top: *Split Rock Lighthouse.*

Facing page, top: *Bunchberry patch.*
Bottom: *The Witch Tree is sacred to area Native Americans. Lake Superior at Grand Portage.*

97

yard. Near the top of a wooded hillside above his home, a large doe kept a suspicious eye on Krueger and on the white bucket that dangled enticingly from his fingertips.

"Come on. Come on," Krueger called to the deer while gently shaking the bucket of corn and alfalfa.

The deer walked cautiously down the wooded hillside, not wanting to get too close to Krueger too fast. Two other deer suddenly appeared in the woods well behind the doe. Then two more off to the east. And another, straight up the hill from Krueger's largest garage.

They all walked carefully and suspiciously down the hill as Krueger filled small wooden troughs with feed. The first deer craned its neck toward the bucket that Krueger was still holding. But she pulled back just before her nose poked inside the white plastic.

"Awful jumpy this year. They don't trust anyone," Krueger said, blaming their mood on packs of wolves.

"They just keep coming. Isn't it amazing," he asked, grinning. "That's Timid over there. That's what I call her, anyway. Look at the horns on that one. All velvet. Just starting to come out.

"Come on big buck. Come on lazy buck."

The buck ate some hay but ignored Krueger's corn and alfalfa mix.

In all, nine deer nosed around at Krueger's feet. Some ate straight from his hand, the way animals always do in those animated Disney movies.

But this was reality, a scene as uniquely North Shore as commercial fishing boats or the jagged Sawtooth Mountains.

"As long as you feed them they'll come around," said Krueger, who has been helping deer survive harsh North Shore winters for more than 20 years. Some years, as many as 125 deer have counted on his kindness. Other years he's fed as few as 20 or 25.

He's not alone. There's a handful of North Shore residents who have been feeding deer for decades. Krueger himself took over for a neighbor who fed deer more than 20 years and could tell you the life history and family tree of every animal who visited his yard.

"Old George over there, he had a name for every single one of them," Krueger said. "Sadly, though, he lost his wife over the whole deal. He paid more attention to the deer than he did to his own house."

Like Marion Calph, Steve Krueger moved to the North Shore from the Twin Cities.

He was born in Minneapolis in 1923. His father was the first assistant secretary to the Minnesota Senate and ached for each opportunity to drive up the North Shore to fish for trout. The elder Krueger also ran the old North Shore Hotel, allowing young Steve to help out during summer vacations.

Steve Krueger flew bombers during World War II, and returned to the North Shore afterward to help his father run the hotel. In 1969, the two men built Chateau LeVeaux, a resort-turned-condominium retreat nestled along the rugged shores of Lake Superior near Tofte.

"I went back to Minneapolis for a short time, but I couldn't see staying down there," said Krueger, who married a North Shore native and passed up a better paying job for the chance to live next to the calming waters of Lake Superior.

In 1969, Krueger moved his family into a two-story home across the highway from the lake. A wide deck offers breathtaking views and a man-made pond in the front yard is home to several ducks.

Krueger restores antique cars, drives a school bus, dabbles in local government—and tends to his deer. There are no traffic jams, no streetlights and no crime. Life is easy, the way it should be.

Inside Krueger's largest garage, there's a sticker he stuck to the wall that uses a heart in place of the word "love." The sticker reads simply: "I ❤ Lake Superior's North Shore."

"I just like it better up here," Krueger said. "I got 20 acres, nobody's moving in close to me and life's a little slower paced. I like that.

"Who wouldn't?"

Duluth's Future

Dan Russell took a lot of ribbing when he moved north to Duluth back in 1979.

Not surprising. The city was plummeting toward rock bottom at the time. Unemployment was near 15 percent. Factories throughout the city's western neighborhoods had shut down. The air base was gone. And mining on the Iron Range to the north was about to come to a standstill, sending shock waves through other local industries, including mainstays like shipping, trucking and railroading.

Stores along Superior Street were closed and rental space was plentiful. You could barely give away your house, let alone sell it.

"Things were so awful," recalled Russell, who moved to Duluth to run the city's convention and visitor's bureau. "The city really did hit a low point in 1980 or 1981.

"But that was also when we realized this is a jewel we're sitting on here," he said. "It's a beautiful city—probably the most beautiful city in the Midwest."

Figuring they could turn things around if they could attract tourists, city leaders turned their sights to Duluth's blue lake and green and granite hills.

Over the next 10 years, using mostly federal highway money, city leaders laid bricks on downtown streets and installed old-fashioned lighting fixtures. They remodeled the old brewery, Fitger's, and turned it into a hotel and a series of specialty shops. On the waterfront and in Canal Park, they refurbished unsightly old warehouses and turned them into handsome shops and cafes.

The extension of Interstate

> *City leaders turned their sights to Duluth's blue lake and green and granite hills. This is a jewel we're sitting on here, a beautiful city—probably the most beautiful city in the Midwest.*

35 went through, and a wooden lakefront walkway was opened. Skywalks were built, linking many of the major downtown buildings with the new Duluth Entertainment Convention Center complex.

The face-lift apparently worked. More than 3.5 million visitors a year now come to Duluth to gawk and spend money and drop compliments. And when they return home, they spread the word that Duluth is back, just as city leaders hoped they would.

The city has seen a rebirth. Call it Duluth's renaissance, now the key to the city's future.

New businesses have already started moving to the more attractive town, in part, to offer their workers a better quality of life. Doctors, professors and other professionals have followed, many yearning for Duluth's slower pace, lack of congestion, recreational opportunities and small-town values.

They're some of those same people who gave Dan Russell a hard time 15 or so years ago.

"Back then when you said you were moving to Duluth, you got some strange looks. Now people are envious that you live up here," Russell said. "The town really did pick itself up by its bootstraps. Not a lot of communities have done that or could do that. I think Duluth is in a position to really take advantage of its attributes now."

Duluth has wisely divorced itself from the old notion that big, blue-collar smokestack industries are the key to a city's success. Large employers—like the air base or U.S. Steel—simply don't exist in the quantity they used to. Here or anywhere.

Encouraging and helping small locally owned businesses spells success nowadays, city leaders have realized.

"Communities in the future

Top: *The Bulldogs pack the house.*
Above: *Petting an emu at the Duluth Zoo.*
Left: *Work is play.*

Facing page: *Boundary Waters Canoe Area Wilderness.*

that have been able to diversify their economic base will flourish," said Marc Mansfield, director of the Duluth Chamber of Commerce. "Those communities that can't will probably die."

Duluth, with its growing number of smaller, high-tech businesses, should survive, its leaders believe.

"In some respects, we're recession proof," Mayor Gary Doty said. "If one part of the economy is down, another will pick it up. We don't want to have to put all of our eggs into one basket anymore. We have bounced back."

Doty was born in Duluth's working class West Hillside neighborhood and grew up in Hunter's Park back when a high school graduate could still land a good-paying job in a factory, on the docks or on a Great Lakes freighter.

Two of his seven brothers and sisters moved away to pursue jobs they couldn't find in Duluth, an early indication of changing times.

One sibling has recently purchased a retirement home here, however, an indication that times are changing again. This time for the better.

"They would both love to be back here," said Doty, a former school teacher.

The rest of the family lives within three miles of each other.

"I'm fortunate to have been able to stay here. I'm fortunate that I was raised here, and I'm for-tunate to raise my own family here. We've got everything here to offer to a family now.

"It's a big enough community to have the advantages of a big city. For example, having our own orchestra or having our own play-house," Doty said. "But it's not like in a city of a million people where you can walk up and down the streets all day and not see anyone you know and wind up feeling insignificant. Duluth is small enough where you can walk down the street and know people. That makes it a friendly community. You can feel significant and make a difference here."

Some say Duluth is the biggest small town in America. "People know each other," Police Chief Scott Lyons said.

"There's not much that happens that we don't hear about." That helps keep crime rates low.

"I wouldn't say we're lowest, but we're definitely middle to lower," Lyons said. "In Duluth, I don't recall the last time we had a murder where we didn't convict somebody. Our success rate in solving crimes, big crimes, is very good."

Unlike other urban centers, Duluth hasn't been plagued by serial attackers or criminals who strike randomly. There's little drug trafficking and only recently have there been whispers of gang activity.

"We get a lot of kids talking about it," Lyons said. "Occasional-ly we see a groundswelling, but then it usually fades away. For the most part, we don't see it."

More than anything, Duluth is a center. Always has been. At one time, it was the passing through point for Great Lakes voyageurs eager to find water passages to the West and South. Later, it was the link between the settled, civilized East Coast and the frontier West.

Today, Duluth is a hub for all of northeastern Minnesota, north-western Wisconsin and large parts of Canada and Michigan's Upper Peninsula. Shoppers crowd Duluth's stores each weekend. And during the week, they fill doctors' offices, concert halls, or the baseball stadium.

Many come just to relax—to let Lake Superior help them refocus and put their lives back into perspective.

And, as more and more people flee the crime and pollution in big cities, more of them will follow Dan Russell's lead and come to Duluth to stay.

"Duluth has always been kind of larger than life to me," Russell said. "Everything we do here is on a big scale. The lake is huge. The hills are high. And the grain elevators are tall. I hope we have the guts to keep doing it up big.

"I hope the city doesn't sit on its laurels now. We need to keep up the energy. If we do, we can go a long way."

Bustling Superior Street in 1916. In the the early 1980s, the city was at a low, with storefronts along Superior Street boarded up and rental space plentiful. Now the city is again thriving, and the residents intend to keep it that way.

Above: *Don't leave Duluth without letting Skyline Parkway lead you to Enger Tower for a spectacular view of your surroundings.*
Top: *A perfect day for a a stroll along the pier at Canal Park.*
Right: *On the waterfront.*

Above: *Taking on cargo.*
Top left: *At rest.*
Left: *The awakening.*

For Further Reading

Abodaher, David J. *Daniel Duluth: Explorer of the Northlands.* N.Y. Kenedy, 1966.

Banning, Margaret Culkin. *Hunter's Park as the Century Turned.* Self published.

Cook, Sam. *CampSights.* Pfeifer-Hamilton, 1992.

Cook, Sam. *If This is Mid-Life, Where's the Crisis?* Pfeifer-Hamilton, 1993.

Cook, Sam. *Quiet Magic.* Pfeifer-Hamilton, 1989.

Cook, Sam. *Up North.* Pfeifer-Hamilton, 1986.

Coventry, William D. *Duluth's Age of Brownstone.* St. Louis County Historical Society, 1987.

Duluth Commemorative Book Committee. *Duluth: 300 Years.* 1979.

Duluth: Research and Planning Office. *Duluth's Legacy: Architecture.* 1974.

Ensign, J.D. *History of the Duluth Harbor.* Ensign, 1898.

Eubank, Nancy. *The Zenith City of the Unsalted Sea.* The Division, 1991.

Everest, Georgia. *Village of Lakeside.* Self published, 1953.

Fedo, Michael. *Chronicles of Aunt Hilma and Other East Hillside Swedes.* North Star Press of St. Cloud, 1991.

Fedo, Michael. *Trial by Mob.* Theatre in the State Inc., 1993.

Fritzen, John. *Historic Sites and Places of Minnesota's North Shore.* St. Louis County Historical Society, 1974.

Fritzen, John. *History of Duluth Heights.* 1980.

Fritzen, John. *History of Fond du Lac and Jay Cooke State Park.* St. Louis County Historical Society, 1978.

Fritzen, John. *History of North Shore Lumbering.* St. Louis County Historical Society, 1968.

Fritzen, John. *Portages and Old Trails in and Adjacent to Jay Cooke State Park,* 1935.

Gullion, Gordon. *Grouse of the North Shore.* Oshkosh: Willow Creek Press, 1984.

Hereid, Nancy and Eugene D. Gennaro. *A Family's Guide to Minnesota's North Shore.* Minnesota Sea Grant, 1993.

Hertzel, Laurie, editor. *Discover Duluth: Boomtown Landmarks.* Pfeifer-Hamilton, 1993.

Kimball, Joe. *Secrets of the Congdon Mansion.* Minneapolis: Jaykay, 1985.

Knopp, Timothy B. *The North Shore Experience.* Minnesota Sea Grant, 1983.

Lund, Duane R. *The North Shore of Lake Superior: Yesterday and Today.* Cambridge, MN: Adventure Publications, 1993.

Lydecker, Ryck and Lawrence J. Sommer, editors. *Duluth: Sketches of the Past: a Bicentennial Collection.* American Revolution Bicentennial Commission, 1976.

Macdonald, Dora Mary. *This is Duluth.* Duluth Central High School Printing Department, 1950.

Macrae, Jean M. *Development of the Glen Avon–Hunter's Park Area of Duluth.* St. Louis County Historical Society, 1961.

Murray, John. *Lake Superior, Wow!* Marlor Press Inc., 1993.

O'Brien, Susan K. *The North Shore.* Fire on the Rocks Publications, 1992.

Sandvik, Glenn. *Duluth: An Illustrated History of the Zenith City.* Windsor Publications, 1983.

Steinke, Jay. *Superior's North Shore.* Tea Table Books, 1993.

Tormondsen, Chris, as told to Bill Westpahl. *Tofte.* Minneapolis: Hayward-Court Brief Printing Co., 1968.

Van Brunt, Walter, editor. *Duluth and St. Louis County: The Story and People* (Volumes 1, 2 and 3). American Historical Society, 1921.

Weiland, Otto E. *Some Facts and Incidents of North Shore History.* North Shore Historical Society, 1937.

Westman, Jim. *The Booster Book: West Duluth Celebrating 100 Years Since Its Union with the City of Duluth.* Unpublished research.

Woodbridge, Dwight E. and John S. Pardee, editors. *History of Duluth and St. Louis County* (Volumes 1 and 2). C.F. Coper, 1910.

Index

Italics indicate illustration

A

Aerial Ferry Bridge 18
Aerial Lift Bridge 18–19, *2, 19, 57, 105, 108*
Algonquin 87
All Sports Stadium. *See* Wade Stadium
American Fur Company 32–34
Amity River Rapids *66*
Armistice Day Snowstorm of 1940 77
Astor, John Jacob 32

B

Bailey, Anne Stultz 54
Barker's Island 94
Bayfront Blues Festival *14*, 15
Bayfront Festival Park 15–16
Beargrease Sled Dog Marathon *75*
Bell, J.B. 54
Belville 54
Blegen, Theodore C. 31
Boundary Waters Canoe Area Wilderness *100*
Brownstone
    buildings 15, 42
    quarrying 42–47
Burnham, Daniel 13

C

Cadotte, Jean Baptiste 32
Caldwell, Roger 26
Calph, Marion 95
Canadian immigrants 54
Canal Park *6*, 18–19, *57, 85*, 99, *104*
Canal Park Marine Museum 86
Canal Park Visitors Center 19
Cargill elevators *41*
Castle Danger 95
Central Administration Building. *See* Old Central High School
Central Entrance 62
Chambers, Michael E. 47
Chester Bowl 27
Christenson, Jim 72
City of Winnipeg steamer 87
Civic Center 13
Climate 72–80
College of St. Scholastica *109*
Company towns 55
Congdon, Chester A. 24, 26
Congdon Creek Falls *56*
Congdon, Elisabeth 26
Connor's Point 94
Cooke, Jay 34–35, 47
Copper mining 34
Coventry, William D. 47
Cowell's Addition 54
Curling 17
Curtis, Chuck 77–79

D

Dakota Indians 30–31
DECC. *See* Duluth Entertainment Convention Center
Depot, The 10, *12, 45*
Doty, Gary 102
Downtown Lakewalk *8*
Dryke, Rosalyn 72
Du Lhut, Sieur (Daniel Greysolon) 30, *31*, 50
Duluth Arena-Auditorium Complex 16
Duluth Art Institute 10
Duluth City Hall 13
Duluth Daily Tribune 47
Duluth Dukes 8–10
Duluth Entertainment Convention Center 16–18, *29*, 63, 99
Duluth Heights 62
Duluth Herald 77
Duluth Herald building 15
Duluth Minnesotian 35
Duluth, Missabe & Iron Range Railway Co. (DM&IR) 8
Duluth News-Tribune 39, 72, 76, 83, 86
Duluth Park Board 68
Duluth Playhouse 10
Duluth Rowing Club 22
Duluth Ski Club 27
Duluth-Superior Dukes 10, 91
Duluth-Superior Symphony Orchestra 10, 17, 91

E

East Hillside 27, 54
Edmund Fitzgerald 17
Ely, Edmund F. 50
Endion 54
Enger, Bert 27
Enger Tower 27–28, *104*
Essex 86
Ethnic groups 54–55
Everest, Georgia 59

F

Fairlawn Mansion Museum *92*, 94
Fero 90
Finnish immigrants 54
Fishing 30
Fitger, August 22
Fitger's Brewery 22–23, *44*
Fond du Lac 30, 39, 47, 50, *51*
Fremont 54
French immigrants 54
Fritzen, John 62
Fur trading 30–34

G

Gary-New Duluth 55
German immigrants 54
Gidley, Joanne 91

JACK RENDULICH

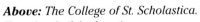

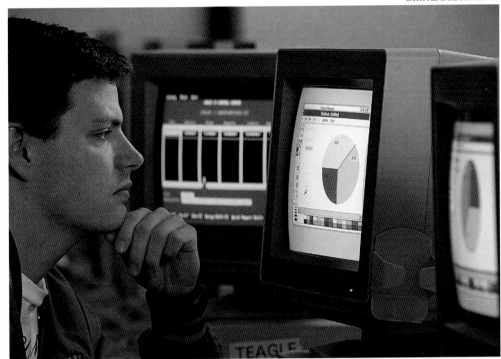

Above: *The College of St. Scholastica.*
Top: *A colorful education.*

Facing page: *The pink moon at the start of a total eclipse goes nicely with the Aerial Bridge.*

Glen Avon 59
Glensheen *14, 24,* 26, *53*
Goat Hill 50
Grand Avenue 5, 7, 8
Grand Portage 32, *33,* 95
Grandma's *45*
Grandma's Marathon *48*
Great Lakes
    shipping 17–18, 19
Great Lakes Towing Company 83
Greenbelt 65
Guido Pfister 86

H

Hatchery 26
Hawk Ridge 26, 27
Hertzel, Laurie 18
Highland Street Car Line 62
History 30–39
Hockey 17
Hog Island 94
Holstrom, Carl 27
Homstad, Joan and Mark 39
Hudson's Bay Company 32
Hunter, James and Ronald 63
Hunter's Park 59

I

Incline Railway 35, *38,* 62
Ingalls, Edmund 47
Irvin, William A., freighter *16,* 17–
    18, 90
Irving 55

J

Jewish immigrants 54
John Beargrease Sled Dog Mara-
    thon *75*
Johnson, George D. 55

K

Kessler, George 76
Kimball, Jerry 65
Kitchi Gammi Club 23
Klees, Joyce 95
Kotlarek, George 27
Krause, Charles A. 47
Krueger, Steve 95–98

L

Labadie, Pat 86, 87
Lake Place Park 22
Lake Superior
    climate 72–80
    geology 26
    shipwrecks 83
Lake Superior and Mississippi
    Railroad 34, 90
Lake Superior Museum *25*
Lake Superior Paper Industries 5
Lake Superior Zoological Gardens
    7
Lake Vermilion 62
Lakeside 26, 54
Lakewalk *8*
Lester Park 26
Lester River 26, *60, 97*
Lewis, Sinclair 26
Lincoln Park 55
Line, Hugh 77
Lumber industry 34, 35
Lyons, Scott 102

M

McCulloch, Hugh 59
McFarlane, Angus 63
Magney, C.R. 68
Mansfield, Marc 102
Marine Museum 19
Mataafa steamer *82,* 86
M.C. Neff 86

Mendenhall, Luther 68
Merritt, Alfred 34
Meteor 94
Middleton 54
Mineral exports 8
Minnesota Ballet 10, 17
Minnesota Canal and Harbor
    Improvement Committee 90
Minnesota Point 18, 19–22, *21,* 30,
    47, *67, 83*
Minor, Dave 91
Morgan, J.P. *6*
Morgan Park 5–7, 35, *49,* 55, *58*
Museums 17–18

N

Neighborhoods 50–63
    Canal Park 18–19
    Central Hillside 50, 54
    Congdon Park 50
    Denfeld 50
    downtown 10–18
    eastern 23–26, 54
    Endion 50, 54
    Fond du Lac 30, 39, 50
    Goat Hill 50
    Lakeside 26, 54
    Lester Park 26
    Minnesota Point 19–22
    Morgan Park 5–7, 35, 55, *58*
    Raleigh Street 50
    Riverside 7, 35, 55
    West Duluth 7, 55
    West End 10
Nemadji River 94
North Duluth 54
North Shore 32, 35, 95–98
North Shore Scenic Railroad 10
Northern Baseball League 10
Northern lights *61*
Northland Vietnam Veterans
    Memorial 22, *41*
Norwegian immigrants 27, 54

O

Oden 87
Ojibwe Indians 30, 31–32, *32*
Old Central High School 7, 42, *44*
Old Vermilion Trail 62
Oliver Bridge 86
Oneota 50–54
Onsgard, Bert 7
Ordean Junior High School
    Stadium *75*

P

Paine Williams, Anne 65–68
Paleo-Indians 30–31
Panic of 1873 47
Park Point 27, *49*
Parks *60*, 65–69
Pattison, Martin 94
Pfeffer, Bernie 38
Pioneer Hall 17
Playfront 15–16
Point of Rocks 10, 50
Polish immigrants 54
Port Byron 54
Portland 54
Portland Malt Shoppe 23
Portland Square 54

R

Reitan, Cheryl and Hugh 63
Rice's Point 54
Riverside 7, 35, 55
Rogers, W.K. 68
Russell, Dan 99, 102

S

St. Louis Bay 8
St. Louis County Courthouse 13
St. Louis County Heritage and
    Arts Center 10, *12, 45*

St. Louis River 34
    and North West Company 32
    neighborhoods 5, 28, 30, 50–54
    shipwrecks 86
    shipyards 35, 55
    transport 47
St. Scholastica, College of *109*
Salter, C.C., Rev. 7
Sandvik, Glenn 35
Scandinavian immigrants 62
Scottish immigrants 63
Shefchik, Thomas 15
Shipbuilding 35–38
Shipping 7–8, 19
Shipwrecks 17, 83–87
Skiing 27
Skyline Parkway 26, 27, 68
Smith, Fred 54
Smithville 55
Snively, S.F. 65–68
Socrates 83–86
Spirit Mountain 7, *66*
Split Rock Lighthouse *97*
Stillman Witt 87
Streetcars 59
Strickland Park 69
Strickland, William W. 69
Stuntz, George R. 62
Sundew 22
Superior Street *11, 103*
Superior, Wisconsin 90–94, *93*
Superior-Douglas County Cham-
    ber of Commerce 91
Swedish immigrants 54, 55

T

Taconite 8
Tettegouche State Park *11*
Thomas E. Wilson steamer 87
Tischer Creek 26
Torrey Building 35
Tourism 39
Tweed Museum of Art 27

Twin Ports 90
Two Harbors 10, 95

U

U.S. Army Corps of Engineers 19
U.S. Coast Guard 22
U.S. Steel 6–7, 17, 35–38, 55
University of Minnesota-Duluth 27
University of Minnesota-Duluth
    Bulldogs 17, *101*

V

Victory Chimes *41*
Vietnam Memorial 22, *41*
Village of Lakeside 59–62

W

Wade, Frank 8
Wade Stadium 8–10, *14*
Walsh, Tom 76
Watson, Bruce 76
West Duluth 7, 55
West End 10
Westman, Jim 55–59
Wheeler, Henry 42
William A. Irvin. See *Irvin, William
    A.*
Willard Munger Trail 7
William Crooks, The *12*
Winslow passenger boat 86
Witch Tree area *96*
Works Progress Administration
    (WPA) 7

Z

Zoo 7, *101*

About the Author

Growing up in suburban Milwaukee, Chuck Frederick used to yearn for the solitude and beauty that only seems to be found "Up North." Writing for the Duluth News-Tribune *has given him the chance to live near his dream. An outdoor and sports enthusiast—and still an avid fan of Wisconsin sports teams—he lives in Duluth's West End with his wife.*

Duluth-Superior Harbor as a new day colorfully begins.